NOT PULLING STRINGS

An Exploration of Music and Instrumental Teaching

Joseph O'Connor

LAMBENT BOOKS

First published 1987
By Lambent Books, London

Copyright © 1987 Joseph O'Connor

Reprinted 1997, 1999

O'Connor, Joseph
Not Pulling Strings: An exploration of music and instrumental teaching using Neuro-Linguistic Programming.
1.   Music—Instruction and study
2.   Neuro-Linguistic Programming
I. Title
780'.7'7   MT 1

ISBN 0-9512155-0-7

Cover design   Andrew Popkiewicz
Cover illustration   Julie Anderson

Printed in Great Britain by J. W. Arrowsmith Ltd, Bristol

Contents

Prelude

This is a book about learning and teaching music. Learning and teaching are abstract nouns and much discussion of them is theoretical. I hope this book is of practical use to all who are involved in music education.

I work as a classical guitar teacher, so I use examples that are taken mostly from my own lessons but, as the book is about the wider process of learning and teaching music, it is relevant to all instruments and of interest, I hope, to all involved in education.

Music is a source of great joy, but sometimes the music lesson is not. S. Suzuki has described the patience of teachers in a wonderfully evocative phrase, as "controlled frustration". This definition eloquently conjures up the feeling teachers may have when trying hard to push knowledge into a student whose head and fingers do not seem to be the right shape to receive it.

Many lessons go very well and I do not want to give the impression that teaching is always concentrating on problems and difficulties. My basic purpose in this book is to expand a teacher's choice of possible methods, so he in turn can give the student more choices. I believe learning is basically expanding your area of choice in what you do and how you do it. Teachers and students are both learners from a wider point of view, they only differ in exactly what they are learning.

Teaching has an overall purpose (the "why"), as well as a number of short-term goals (the "what"). My overall purpose in teaching the guitar is to allow my students to become more competent and independent, and feel enjoyment and confidence. I will have many different short-term goals, mostly concerned with increasing the students' musical skills and instrumental technique. People do things and continue doing things that make them feel good. They ultimately learn for their own reasons, not for the reasons of others. Teaching that loses sight of its purpose by getting caught up in its goals is liable to generate Suzuki's "controlled frustration".

The process (the "how") of achieving these goals must keep the overall purpose in mind to be effective and enjoyable. Having decided the goals, it is a matter of being sensitive in the present moment to what is happening in the lesson, and flexible enough to change methods if what you are doing is not working. It may appear in this account that I always said and did the right thing, but there were many times when I did not. I just kept trying different ideas until I found one that worked with a particular student.

Some ways of teaching work well for some students but not for others. The keen, talented student who practises regularly is easy to teach; he or she virtually takes care of him or herself. Others may struggle, despite going through the same teaching process that worked for their classmate. They do not learn in the same way. These students are the most valuable, they force a teacher to reappraise his approach and try something different, he must be creative.

Any approach to learning that does not take the student as the starting point is like mistaking a mirror image for an actual object and trying to deduce the laws of optics from it. Everything is back-to-front.

This book explores the application of Neuro-Linguistic Programming (NLP) to teaching. NLP was developed by Richard Bandler and John Grinder in America from 1975 and is having an increasing influence in business, law and education all over the world. It is basically a model of how individuals use their senses in communicating and acquiring skills, and how they structure their subjective experience. It shows how people make sense of what they see, hear and feel.

NLP began by investigating how exceptionally talented people at the top of their profession were able to achieve their extraordinary results. The techniques they used became the working principles of NLP. One of its strengths is the possibilities it gives for modelling, or copying and reproducing excellence in any field. Successful and talented people use certain ways of working. This is precisely why they are successful and talented. NLP makes these strategies visible, tangible and audible so that they can be taught to others.

NLP focuses on individual experience and is directly useful to teachers for it allows them to understand and gain rapport with their students and give knowledge to each in the best way. Because NLP is concerned only with the process of learning, it can be applied to all subjects.

I will outline some of the main ideas of NLP and give practical examples of how they can be applied to aural memory, mental rehearsal and learning how to read music. I will give a general model of how music is learnt, as a starting point for discussion and elaboration.

Language is the main way we communicate ideas but it can never do complete justice to our thoughts, misun-derstanding is bound to occur. Students will also indi-cate by their use of language where they believe their limitations lie. I have given a brief account in chapter two of the NLP Meta Model, which is specifically designed to clear up the ambiguities of language.

"Practice" is another abstract noun, and I have tried to show what it means to students in reality, and how to form useful practice habits.

This book is incomplete in the sense that I could write a much better and fuller account in a few years   time, when I would have gained more experience and knowledge, but the same criticism would apply whenever I wrote, or whoever was writing. The more we know, the more questions are generated and this will always be so. The more we know, the more ignorant we become, or at least the more we are aware of our lack of knowledge. So this book is not meant to be a once-and-for-all statement on learning for myself, or anyone else.

I have used masculine and feminine pronouns at random when talking about students and teachers, this is purely for ease of communication and to avoid unwieldy sentence construction.

I like the metaphor of the teacher as a magician. He has

arcane skills and knowledge and can do musical miracles in the student's eyes. The student will want to be the sorcerer's apprentice, it is as if he gives his talents and potential to the teacher for safe keeping and development. The teacher's work is to demystify himself and give back with interest what the student has loaned him. NLP can give the teacher seemingly magical skills of communication to help in this task.

I would like to thank many people who gave me ideas or practical help for this book; John Paynter, John Sloboda, Morris Kahn, John Seymour, Doug Huxtable, John Canning. Andrew Popkiewicz, Leora Gaster, John Kopecky and my father.

I would particularly like to thank Gilbert Biberian, Julian Goodburn, Karen Wentworth and Eloise Ristad for sharing their knowledge with me, so that I could use it in my own way.

Finally, I owe a debt to my students for giving me the opportunity to learn so much. They tolerated many seemingly pointless questions about how they practised, how they visualised and how they accomplished other, non-musical tasks. My thanks to them too for so often being patient when I did not, or was slow to understand what they were showing me.

Chapter One

Teaching and Learning

Teaching is the art of communicating knowledge and skills from one person to another. Learning is building up and connecting knowledge and skills with what is already known. It increases the range of choices available in any field of activity, when you learn something new you have widened your awareness. You now have another, possibly better way to do something.

I work as a teacher of the classical guitar, so I need tc pass on knowledge and build up the musical skills of my students. As their technique and musicianship improves, they will be able to play more music; eventually they will take responsibility for their own learning completely. I am successful as a teacher to the degree my students become musically self-sufficient.

The teacher is a learner too. Each student brings his or her own unique personality and talents to a lesson and these will illuminate aspects of music the teacher may not have considered. Each student is an unprecedented opportunity for the teacher to learn something new. By coming to understand different students and the way they learn, he can expand his range of methods to communicate knowledge and expertise clearly and appropriately.

Communication involves the interaction of two people. It is a word which, like the Roman God Janus, faces in two directions. At a basic level, communication is a cycle. The teacher says or demonstrates something and this draws an internal response from the student, who will think about what he has seen and heard and act accordingly. The teacher will see and hear the student's external responses and will react internally with his own thoughts, feelings and images, preparing for his next action, which in turn will evoke an internal response from the student. And so the cycle continues.

To take a practical example, I might describe and

demonstrate the note on the third string, second fret of
the guitar and ask the student to play it. He may respond
by putting his finger in the correct place. If he puts his
finger on string four, fret two, then I have not got my
message across. Seeing this, I may respond by repeating
what I said, or by actually moving his finger. This is a
straightforward example, but it does illustrate an important point. The student may have forgotten that the
strings are numbered from the bottom upwards and may
be counting from the top downwards, so he may think
that his finger is actually on string three.

If I simply   repeat   my instruction, he may not
understand what he is doing wrong, even if I manually
move his finger he still may not deduce his   error.
However, by realising how the strings are numbered, he
can correct his own mistake, so it is important   to understand the inner response, as well as the outer behaviour.

To be an effective teacher, I have to appreciate how
he is thinking and   enter   his world. I must fit my explanation to his way of learning and his present understanding; where music is exciting and unfamiliar. I need
to recognise the processes he uses to make sense of the
information that I give him. I must meet him on his own
ground so both of us can begin the journey. He cannot
meet me at my level.

Music teachers need rapport with their students and
an understanding of the methods they use to gain musical skills. I want to outline how teachers can more easily
appreciate and understand what their students are
experiencing, their inner response as well as the outer
behaviour, and help them to achieve   their goals. To this
end, I want to explore some ideas about how we think
that will give a useful map of the structure of subjective
experience. I invite you to consider a very interesting and
useful way of thinking about experience. It is a map, so it
is not true and complete, just as a map is not a true and
complete representation of what it covers. But it is
invaluable for getting you to your destination.

Sense Experience

Each of us has a model of the world built up during our life from our unique and personal experience. Our sensory perceptions ultimately determine how the world appears to us. Vision, touch, taste, smell and hearing provide us with the raw material with which we build our version of reality. We certainly all agree broadly about the way the world is, but people think and feel very differently about the same experience (listening to a Beethoven quartet for example, or walking in the rain, or the taste of meat). No-one knows what the world is really like, although we all have beliefs about it. As Shakespeare said, "There is nothing either good or bad, but thinking makes it so."

We choose to be conscious of only a small fraction of the diverse sounds, sights, smells, tastes and contacts that we have every moment. Our senses are bombarded with information all the time; it has to be filtered, sorted and given a high or low priority for attention depending on our interests at that particular moment. Our senses tend to respond most acutely to changes in the environment. We can become so used to a familiar sight, sound or feeling that we simply cease to notice it. It is recognised and taken for granted. New experience engages our attention.

Internal Senses

We can recall our sense experience and recreate it in our mind from memory. We can also imagine sights, feelings, tastes, smells and sounds that we have not actually experienced. We have an internal proprioceptive sense of touch which provides us with feedback about our movements, without it we could not control our bodies as they move around in space. I will refer to awareness of any bodily sensations as the kinaesthetic sense and this will include the internal sense of touch, as well as emotions and other bodily feelings. Just as we use our five senses outwardly to "present" the world to ourselves, we can also use them inwardly to "re-present" our sense experience to ourselves, hence the five senses when used internally are known as representational systems; visual, auditory, kinaesthetic, olfactory and gustatory.

Imagine yourself lying on a beach on a tropical island. Picture the beach and the palm trees all around, and imagine the intense reflection of the sun from the sand, dazzling your eyes. Can you hear the roar of the surf and the shouts of the swimmers as they splash in the shallows? Can you hear the exotic birds calling, and the busy rustle of insect life chattering to itself further up the dunes in the long grass? Can you feel the sun beating down on your back, and the sand between your toes? There is a beach barbecue nearby. Can you smell the meat sizzling on the spit, and taste the salt water on your lips?

We can all "use the imagination" like this. This is using the senses inwardly to represent the world to ourselves. If you have experienced certain sights, sounds and feelings, then you can recall them directly from memory. If you have not, then you will construct them from your life experiences, building a mosaic where the bricks are familiar, but the end result is a new creation. For example, if you have experienced the sights, sounds and feelings that I described on the tropical island, you can draw on these memories directly, and they will be quite specific (and different from my specific visual, auditory and sensual memories). If you have not had a direct experience, then you will build a composite picture and create the sounds and feelings from other sources, perhaps from books, films, or similar resources.

When we inwardly represent our experience, the same neural pathways are used as when we sense outwardly. Thoughts have direct physical effects too. Thinking about eating a lemon will cause salivation and thinking of a bad experience can make you wince. Our thoughts are intimately linked with bodily states. It is impossible to treat them separately in any meaningful way. Internal and external responses form a unity.

These internal senses are not mutually exclusive; pictures can generate the sounds associated with them and in order to remember sensations, it may be necessary to picture the scene first. As a general principle, the more a person is using a sense inwardly as a representational system, the less he can pay attention with it outwardly. Someone who is making pictures in his mind (visualizing), will not notice so much of what is going on in the world outside. The more a person is immersed in his inner world of sights, sounds and feelings, the less he will be aware of the external world. Being "lost in thought" is a familiar sensation.

We are constantly aware of the external world and these sense experiences are remembered and translated into internal representations which govern our behaviour. Each person draws his map of the world from the palette of his personal experience. Just as we can only experience the external world in the first place by using our senses outwardly, so the only way we can represent it to ourselves in retrospect is to use the senses inwardly. These representations form our thoughts which give rise to language - the principal way we communicate what we are thinking to others, although we shall see that body language is very eloquent in its own right.

Our behaviour is a mixture of internal and external sense experience. For example, as I type this, I am aware of the touch of my fingers on the typewriter keys and the sight of the keyboard. I am not primarily aware of the clatter of the keys as I type, unless I specifically think of it. In fact, what I am hearing most of the time is my own internal dialogue, sorting out in advance what I wish to commit to paper. My visual and kinaesthetic senses are being used mostly outwardly, my auditory sense is mostly internal, and my sense of taste and smell are dormant. This would change if I stopped for a moment to visualise a scene which I wanted to describe. I might also hear someone call me, or smell food, which would again change the sensual balance .

These internal sights, sounds and feelings make up our thoughts and they are the most direct or primary way

we represent the world to ourselves. The next step
involves language to transmit our thoughts to others.
Language is a secondary representational system, it is
generated by and dependent on our inner world, yet only
gives a pale reflection of its variety. Everyone has a
slightly (or greatly) different internal experience
associated with the same word, because they have
had slightly (or greatly) different external experiences of
what the word is used to describe. Firstly, there may be
actual physical limits on their sense experience: sharpness
of eyesight, acuteness of hearing and sensitivity of touch.
Secondly, different environments will give different
experiences. Usually the differences between people's
understanding of words are small enough not to matter
very much, but we can never know exactly what another
person is thinking, especially with vague words like
love, learning, skill, ability etc. Language can never do
justice to our primary sense experience. It will attenuate
it and represent only a small portion. Thought is faster
than our ability to put it into words.

Preferred Internal Senses

Different people value and use some senses more
than others. Particular senses may have been trained, or
just naturally be more acute. A wine taster will typically
have a very discriminating palate. A surgeon must have
good eyesight and a sculptor a sensitive touch. We take
this for granted when we think of using our senses
externally.

Internal senses vary in acuteness too, and people differ
in how highly they value them. Many people can make
clear eidetic images, others find it difficult to imagine
pictures. Each person's internal sensual balance will not
be the same as his neighbour's and this means that his
experience, and his description of his experience, and the
recreation of his experience subsequently will be different
from that of his neighbour.

A musician is typically somebody who has a highly

Aural.

developed internal and external auditory sense. He is able not only to hear and enjoy more complex patterns of sound than someone else, but he can also mentally recreate the music internally in the same refined way. This is the "inner ear" of the musician and aural training specifically attempts to improve this. Mozart, while still a young boy, was reputedly able to write a whole complex piece of music from memory after very few hearings. This is an extreme example. Everyone can replay a tune mentally (sometimes tunes just will not go away), though not of course in such detail and clarity as Mozart. A visually oriented person going to a concert would not make the aural distinctions, but might be able to describe the whole environment in detail and could possibly make a detailed drawing of the surroundings afterwards from his visual memory, to the astonishment of the musician.

People differ in the strength and clarity with which they can use their senses internally. Some people can make clear pictures, others can hear sounds distinctly and yet others can imagine feelings very strongly. We have the possibility of using all the representational systems, and everyone uses all of them all the time with more or less awareness of each. One system is no better than another in an absolute sense, but one, or a certain combination, will be more suitable for any given task.

Each person has a most highly valued inner sense or preferred representational system that he typically uses to represent his experience to himself. This system will be clearer and capable of making finer distinctions than the others. In other words some people will think mostly in pictures, others might talk to themselves a great deal, while others will base their actions more on their feelings.

This is a gross simplification of course, but it is a useful general idea. One way of identifying a person's most highly valued representational system, or the one he uses habitually, is to listen to his speech. Since language is thought put into words and thought is based on these systems, he will choose words that best represent his internal experience. Listen to the type of words a person habitually uses, especially the verbs, adjectives and adverbs. These parts of speech are often called predicates in NLP literature.

Some people use visual expressions. They *see* things clearly, *paint* word pictures, and give *vivid images*. This is actually what their thoughts consist of. Others may use auditory words. They will *hear* from people, *call* in, take things *quietly*, or protest *loudly*. Yet others will say they *feel strongly* about issues, make *contact* with people, or be *touched* by events. The perceptive reader can find out from this, or any other book, the author's dominant representational system. These expressions show ways of understanding in a totally literal sense, for language has a direct link with sensory experience. Some words are not sensory-based, and are known as digital predicates. Some people in fact operate mostly with these words, and it is generally accepted that academic books and papers must use mostly digital words, since these seem to be more objective. Unfortunately these words are also the least specific and therefore will be "translated" differently by their auditory, visual and kinaesthetic readers.

Accessing Cues

Sometimes I ask a student to think of the feeling in his left hand fingers while playing a particular chord. He must recreate a feeling, or access that feeling from his store of memories. If I ask a student to form a picture of his left hand on the fingerboard, or to hear the music internally, he will have to use information from a different internal sense. There are clues from body language to indicate which sense is being used internally. We are quite used to interpreting other people's body language, it adds a dimension to what they are saying and how they are feeling. Obvious examples are frowning, scratching the head, clenching the fists and many other similar gestures and postures. However there are more subtle signs, usually unnoticed, giving a wealth of information about how a person is thinking.

Examples of Sensory Based Predicates

Seeing Visual	*Hearing* Auditory	*Feeling* Kinaesthetic	*Smelling* Olfactory
look	say	touch	scented
picture	question	move	stale
bright	accent	handle	fishy
focus	rhythm	contact	nosy
image	sing	grasp	fresh
colour	loud	smooth	smoky
insight	melody	push	fragrant
vivid	tone	rub	
scene	resonate	scratch	
blank	echo	solid	*Tasting*
dazzle	sound	drop	Gustatory
visualise	monotonous	warm	sour
dark	deaf	cold	flavour
perspective	hum	rough	bitter
shine	ring	tackle	taste
reflect	demand	turn	salty
eye	ask	push	juicy

Examples of Non Sensory Based (Digital) Predicates

decide	think	know	understand
calculate	explain	conceptualise	attend
meditate	remember	evaluate	recognise
inform	cognizance	discern	perceive

There are also many sensory based metaphors enshrined in language:

Visual Metaphors	Auditory Metaphors
I see what you mean	Tune in
Can you picture it?	On the right wavelength
I have looked closely at this	Get an earful
Things are looking up	Sounds good
We see eye to eye	It's all Greek to me
He's in a black mood	Music to my ears
I have a hazy idea	Tell me the truth
My mind has gone blank	What is your story?
Quite a spectacle	That rings true
Crystal clear	Ring the changes
He's got a blind spot	Call the tune
Show me what you mean	A face like thunder

Kinaesthetic Metaphors

Stay in contact	A hard case
Thick-skinned	Going to pieces
Skin deep	You've hurt his feelings
A cool customer	Scratch the surface
A luke-warm reaction	Snatch a few moments
Blowing hot and cold	A comfortable situation
Don't be a wet blanket	I can't put my finger on it
Keep in touch	He's a soft touch
Heavy handed	Light as a feather

Olfactory and Gustatory Metaphors

A fishy situation
Smell a rat
What rotten luck
A taste for the good life
A sweet person
An acid comment
A bitter pill
Fresh as a daisy

Patterns of eye movement indicate which sense is being used when a person is accessing information internally in response to any cognitive task (See Figure 1). The direction of eye movement both laterally and vertically seems to be associated with activation of different parts of the brain (Galin and Ornstein 1974, Kinsbourne 1972,73). When we visualise anything in our past experience, our eyes tend to move upwards and to our left. This movement is associated with eidetic images in the right hemisphere of the brain, because the left visual field is represented there. Staring straight ahead or defocusing the eyes, "looking into the distance", also shows visualization. When we try to construct a picture of something that is outside our experience, our eyes tend to move upwards and to the right.

When we recall a sound, voice, or music, our eyes tend to move sideways and to the left. Trying to hear a sound we have never heard before sends our eyes sideways and to the right. Finally, imagining a feeling or physical sensation, our eyes tend to go downwards and to our right. Eye movement downwards and to the left also indicates auditory access, it is characteristic of internal dialogue, or "talking to oneself".

There is some innate neurological connection between these eye movements and the different representational systems, for they have been observed to be the same in individuals belonging to different cultures, and also in people who have been blind from birth. Only the Basque people of Northern Spain seem to have significantly and consistently different patterns.

These are typical eye movements, and hold for the majority of people. There are exceptions, but a person's eye movements will be consistent for that person, even if different from those of everyone else. There is no forced connection for everyone, but, if the eye movements are not consciously controlled, then they will be predictable. We make them quite naturally without thinking. They may also be linked with the rapid eye movements (REM) we make when we are dreaming.

Visual constructed images
*(Dominant   Hemisphere
Visualization)*

Visual remembered images
*(Non-dominant   hemisphere
visualization)*

Constructed sounds
*(Dominant hemisphere
auditory)*

Remembered Sounds
*(Non-dominant   hemisphere
auditory)*

Kinaesthetic
*(Feelings and bodily
sensations)*

Auditory Digital
(Internal   dialogue)

Figure 1

Some people can consciously move their eyes in any direction they wish while thinking in different ways, but accessing is made easier with the appropriate natural eye movements. These eye movements are not necessarily reversed for left-handers. One of my right-handed students does actually reverse every one. Her eyes move right when remembering, and left when constructing.

We can easily become aware of our own characteristic eye movements by paying attention to our thought processes. We can also see the eye accessing cues of others by asking simple questions and paying attention to the eye movements and not the answers. If you find exceptions to the general patterns described, trust your sensory experience and not the fixed formula.

I spent some time verifying these patterns by asking my students various questions. I was not at all interested in the answers, only how they arrived at them. In fact I specifically told them not to tell me the answers, but simply to say when they had an answer. This was extremely useful for me, for it gave me the process each student used to access information. I could use these to check and discover how students remembered musical facts and skills. I should say I only did this when I had good rapport, and I did not make them self-conscious by telling them I was watching their eye movements. It is not necessary to be so organised. It is quite possible to ascertain a person's characteristic eye movements in the course of a normal conversation.

This rapport is important, for it has been shown that lateral eye movements are influenced by the position of the questioner (Gur and Gur 1975). In this study, subjects typically looked to the left or right regardless of the nature of the question, if the experimenter was facing them. When the experimenter was out of sight of the subjects, their eye movements were linked to the question that was asked. A likely explanation is that in an anxiety-provoking "test" situation, subjects are more likely to fall back on habitual responses, regardless of whether they are appropriate to the questions posed.

The following were the sorts of questions I asked to

get eye movements for visual memory:
What does the queen look like on TV?
What is the first thing you see when you wake up in the morning?
What colour is your lounge carpet?
What colour are your mother's eyes?
What colour is your front door?
What did your first instrumental teacher look like?
How many sides has a fifty pence piece?

Questions for visual construction:
What would your bedroom look like with pink and yellow wallpaper?
If a map is upside down, which direction is southeast?
Imagine a blue square in a red circle.
How do you spell your Christian name backwards?
What would you look like in a clown's suit?
Divide 273 by 3.

Questions for auditory memory:
Can you hear your favourite chart record in your mind?
Which door slams loudest in your house?
Listen to a guitar chord in your mind.
Hear the sound of seagulls.
What does circus music sound like?
Hear the sound of your mother's voice in your mind.

Questions for auditory construction:
If Beethoven could give some advice to Bach, what would he say?
Imagine the sound of a piano falling off a cliff.
Imagine the scream of a mandrake.

Kinaesthetic questions
Which is colder, your left hand or your right hand?
What does it feel like when you cut your nails?
Feel your front teeth bite into an ice-cream cone.
What does does it feel like to put on wet socks?
What does it feel like to jump into a swimming pool?
What does silk feel like?

How do you keep your balance with your eyes closed?

Lateral eye movements are not the only indication of which representational system is being used. There are other body language signs. A telephone position is associated with internal dialogue. A person in this position will lean his head on his hand or fist so that it inclines to one side, usually the left. It looks as if he is talking on an invisible telephone. People will often point to their eyes to indicate the visual sense, their ears to indicate auditory access, and their abdomen to show kinaesthetic access. It is taken for granted that people will do this when using the senses externally; for example "I see you", or, "I haven't heard from him", or, "I feel strongly about that", but it also happens when people are accessing internally, in which case they may not say anything to clarify what they are doing. All these accessing cues give no indication whatever of the content of the sight, feeling or sound, only the process involved.

Breathing Changes

A person's breathing will normally change when he concentrates. High, shallow breathing in the chest usually accompanies visual access. Even breathing over the whole chest area, often with a prolonged exhalation, goes with internal dialogue, and deep full breathing from the diaphragm usually indicates kinaesthetic access. These breathing changes will accompany internal or external use of the particular sense.

Lead System

Often the words people use will not match with their accessing cues. When I asked some of my students a question about feelings, they would often look up and to the left, then down and to the right before replying. The lead system is the one a person uses to gain immediate access to information and it may differ from the most valued system shown by the predicates. For example, when I asked some people the auditory question about which door in their house slams the loudest, some would look up to the left first. I took this to mean that they were picturing the doors before comparing how loudly they slammed. Others would look down to the right, the most obvious explanation being that they were imagining the feeling of slamming the doors to compare the sounds. The eventual answer must involve an auditory access, but in the first case the lead system was visual, in the second, kinaesthetic. Typically there was a visual response to the question about Beethoven giving advice to Bach, followed by an auditory one, showing that the picture came before the conversation was imagined. Eye movements will happen very quickly. You need to be very attentive to see them all.

Rapport

Trust is fundamental to a good relationship and essential for effective teaching. Trust comes from the feeling of being understood by the other person. Understanding is the bridge between two different models of the world, each made from unique sense experiences. Understanding is shown by what we say, but body language is the most important way of gaining rapport.

Studies have shown that the words we use account for about 7% of what we communicate to another person. 35% is communicated through our tone of voice and a huge 55% by our physiology and body language. A little reflection on everyday communication will show that this balance is accurate.

The exact figures may be arguable, but clearly our body language, appearance, and tone of voice are far more important than the words we use when we communicate. There must be at least a dozen ways of saying "no", for example, all with slightly different meanings. However elegantly we may express ourselves verbally, and however relevant it may be in the situation, people are unlikely to respond positively to a rough tonality and awkward body language. Actors know this. They are trained in tonality and body language. A good comedian's material may not be so hilarious in the cold light of day: it's the way he tells it. I seriously believe that all teacher training should involve some time at Drama School. (Learning how to be a good stand-up comedian would be the most useful course to take). The way for a teacher to be more effective is to pay attention to his tonality and body language. .

We act differently with different people. We show different faces to our spouses, peers, children and acquaintances. Without this flexibility, life would be embarrassingly difficult. We can further refine our natural ability to respond to the needs of others.

Good relationships depend on good communication. Good communicators naturally put people at ease by entering into their world. They soon establish rapport: they have the ability to make different types of people respond to them. They do this by matching their body language, tonality and words to the person they are with. It is rather like a dance. Dancers will stay in step and move together without actually copying each other; their movements are complementary.

A teacher can create good rapport by matching and pacing some of the student's verbal and non-verbal behaviour. He can match the student's rate and location of breathing and general body posture. Speech patterns and tempo can also be matched. This does not mean obvious, exact and complete imitations of behaviour, but a subtle mirroring of gestures, posture, tonality and movement where appropriate. It is part of being in sympathy with, and understanding the other person. You do not abandon your own characteristic behaviour. It is no different fundamentally from discussing areas of common interest. It does not destroy your own integrity and we take it for granted in our culture that you make eye contact with the person you are talking to.

This matching and mismatching will occur uncon-

sciously anyway. Observation of two people talking together soon   shows if they are in sympathy with one
another. Those who agree and   share an understanding
tend to adopt the same general postures and gestures, and
speak in the same rhythm and tempo. People who are
not in accord will adopt very different attitudes and tend
to interrupt each other's speech. If you wish to get away
from somebody you will automatically and unconsciously
mismatch   gestures and posture and avoid eye contact.
The ultimate mismatch of course, is to turn your back. It
is better to be aware of matching and mismatching,   for
then it becomes a choice. All teachers wish to help and
guide their students, so   there is no pretence involved.
All   teacher   training   emphasises   having   good
relationships with   students,   unfortunately, it never
explains how. Matching body language is the answer.

Learning to match and to be in rapport is best done
slowly, a step at a time, perhaps starting with general
posture and characteristic gestures. Later, volume, rhythm
of speech and breathing rate can be included. The only
limitation is the teacher's behavioural flexibility.

Postural habits of students can be changed by matching
them initially, then gradually changing to a more effective posture. The student will often follow this lead. This
is another choice to providing a clear role model right
from the start and asking the student to copy it.

There are some misunderstandings about listening
that can cause frustration in a lesson. A person with a
preferred visual sense will want to see the speaker to
understand what he is saying. The visual person will
also project this rule onto others and think that they too
must look at him while he is talking, otherwise they
are not listening. He may get upset or angry if he is talking
and the other person is not looking at him. "Look at me
when I'm talking to you!" is said all too often by adults
to children. A person with a dominant kinaesthetic or
auditory sense does not need to look in order to listen, in
fact looking may even distract him. He will need to look
away to use his own dominant sense.

Sometimes   students will stare into the distance, then they need some time to "see" what you are telling them. (They may be bored and be making pictures of something totally different!) It is not worth continuing to explain however. They are making sense of what has gone before: more explanation will simply overload their understanding.

Verbal Pacing

Verbal pacing involves matching predicates with students so there is no contradiction between what you say and the student's internal experience. If the student is predominantly a visualiser, then it is better for the teacher to ask him to "see" something than to "listen" to an explanation. Whatever type of predicate a student uses is the type to use in an explanation or reply. I have had students tell me that they "cannot see how to come to grips with the music". I can then match my explanation to the sequence that my student uses to understand: visual followed by kinaesthetic. Neutral words like "imagine", "think", or "understand" can have different meanings to different people. By changing the form of words they use, teachers will allow students to follow them easily. Once again, you will be matching and mismatching anyway, all the time and it is better to be aware than unaware of what is happening.

A "learning disability" is largely a creation of a system that works in a fixed way. This diagnosis is more likely to be a statement about the relationship between the teacher and the taught, or rather, the teacher's method and the student's understanding. They do not see eye to eye. Perhaps they see eye to ear. It is a failure of communication. This is one reason why a child can do very poorly during one year at school with one teacher and do very well the next with a different one - as long as the second teacher does not believe the initial diagnosis.

NLP and Communication

In this chapter I have tried to introduce some of the key ideas of NLP and indicate how they can be used in teaching. At the same time, these ideas themselves are only a map or model of communication and behaviour. All maps are incomplete, but useful, even invaluable in certain circumstances. NLP is a generalised model of experience. Everyone is different. It is best to have your senses as open as possible and trust what you see, hear and feel. If a map is not useful it is best not to use it.

Representational systems, predicates and rapport are powerful ideas and in the following chapters I intend to apply them more specifically to music and instrumental teaching. In fact rapport is the most important of all, for without this basic trust, teaching and learning is much more difficult, if not impossible.

For good communication, a teacher needs to be very clear about what he wishes to achieve. He must be sensitive enough to see, hear and feel what is happening. He cannot be inside his own head, paying attention to his own internal experience, or he will miss what is actually happening in the present moment. A teacher needs as many choices as possible to achieve the outcome he wishes. The sensory feedback he receives will tell him whether what he is doing is actually working and what to do next. If it is not working, he must do something else, it is pointless to continue doing the same thing as if the student is at fault for failing to understand. A student who does not understand is simply giving feedback about your behaviour.

So, what is the real meaning of any communication? It is the response it gets. I have found working on this principle is fun as well as very effective.

Chapter Two

Language and Teaching

Most teaching is done by verbal explanations and direct demonstration. Students will make their own meanings of what you say and how you say it and often will not understand what you are trying to convey. Quite apart from inherent difficulties in the ideas being explained, they have not made an intelligible "translation" of your explanation into their own vocabulary and experience. Teachers need to look carefully at language as a means of communication to see where it is ambiguous. Language has no "real" meaning as such, what the other person understands is what matters.

Language is essentially a map of our sense experience, which in turn is a model of the world we live in, so language is at second remove from reality. It is a model of a model, or a metamodel. Words can be mistaken for reality, rather like going to a restaurant and eating the menu. The power of words comes from their ability to evoke images, sounds and feelings in the reader or listener, as any poet or advertising copywriter will tell you. Language can be used to enlarge or limit our view of ourselves and our world. It is the shared medium of communication with others in society. As it has a social dimension it will reflect the relative importance of objects and events in that society. For example, the Eskimos have seventy different words for our word "snow". It is important for them to make these distinctions. Their survival may depend on precise identification of the type of snow.

The Hanuoo peoples distinguish between ninety-two different varieties of rice and have a name for each. If this surprises us, they might be equally amazed to hear that we have roughly the same number of words for different types of car. Rice is not important to us, nor motor cars to them.

So the vocabulary of a language is limited or expanded

first of all according to social and environmental conditions. Secondly, the structure of language channels the
way we think about events and how we act. The English language basically uses sentences involving a
subject, predicate and object. Linguistically, subjects are
active and do things to passive objects, but this is a gross
simplification of actual events and there is a danger that
we may come to connect people or events by the way we
think about them linguistically. I am very often writing
about a teacher teaching a student, with the student
learning from the teacher, as if teachers are doing things
to passive students. In reality there is a reciprocal relationship and students are far from passive, they are actively making their own meanings of what the teacher says
in the light of their own experience. On a higher level,
both teacher and student are equal, both are learning, but
about different things. Anyone who thinks that lessons
are a one-way passage of information will be constantly
frustrated.

It is difficult to point out built-in assumptions in
language using the self-same language. By using subjects,
verbs and objects, the English language tends to make us
think in terms of cause and effect, rather than connections
and processes. As I look out of the window, I see the
bushes in the garden being blown by the wind. The
wind 'causes' the branch to bend. This is a useful
simplification, but to understand what is actually
happening, many more things need to be known (What
causes the wind?). You could say the elasticity of the
branch causes it to bend, for if it was more rigid it would
not bend at all. You might also say the branch bending
causes disturbances in the air pressure around it. You
would have to look into botany, atmospherics, elasticity
and aerodynamics for a better understanding of the total
phenomenon. This is the way knowledge progresses.
Men look at events that seem obvious, and ask
questions about them that have not been asked before;
they connect them in a new way to other knowledge.

Over a period of time the reciprocal relationship is
closer to reality than simple cause and effect, otherwise

the chicken and the egg riddle is insoluble. Both chicken and egg are still-life photographs of the same process at different points in time.

The Map is not the Territory

Language is our shared means of communication about sense experience. We connect meanings to words according to our particular and unique sense experiences and each person's experience will be different. Whether we change our point of view, explore new possibilities or ring changes in our lives, it is not the world that changes but our way of perceiving it.

A map is an extremely good metaphor for language. The whole point of a map is that it is useful, manageable and incomplete. It helps to explore new territory. If I were driving to the next town, I would want a simple road map. I would not want a large scale map with details of houses, geographical contours or population density. A demographer however, may want a map with just that type of information. A map that tried to be totally realistic would cover the whole area it was supposed to map and would be indistinguishable from it, so it would be useless as a map.

Language creates understanding between people as well as misunderstanding and the illusion of understanding. To take a simple example: if I tell a friend that I have had an enjoyable holiday, he will search through his own experiences of his enjoyable holidays and perhaps picture me lazing on a sunny beach. If I tell him I have actually been potholing, he might make a picture of himself stuck in a cramped tunnel, wince and question my sanity. If I do not elaborate on the details of my holiday, I might be suprised when he remarks on my suntan (or lack of it). It is not very important here whether my friend understands exactly what I was doing, so I need not be specific, but in another context it may be very important.

We are constantly modifying language for immediacy of communication. Problems come into sharper focus in a lesson because its specific outcome is to create an understanding between the teacher and the student. A teacher's words are generated from his knowledge and experience and a listening student will connect them with his own quite different knowledge and experience. This is quite apart from lapses of attention, clarity of presentation, or mutual inability to grasp certain ideas. The more precisely teachers can use language while appreciating the deletions and distortions necessary for immediate communication, the better chance they will have of reaching a student's understanding.

Deletions, Distortions and Generalizations of Language

Good verbal communication involves both understanding the other person's meaning and phrasing your own ideas in a way he can readily understand. One exercise often used in psychotherapy involves a conversation where a person must paraphrase what another person has just said, to the initial speaker's satisfaction, before he is allowed to reply. "Communication breakdown" is understanding a statement differently from the way it was meant. I should like to consider systematically possible misunderstandings in verbal communication, with particular reference to possible conversations between students and teachers.

As language is an approximation of our inner sensory experience, it will leave out, or delete information, often because what is left out is assumed to be obvious. It may be obvious to the speaker, but not to the listener. Secondly a speaker may unwittingly distort his meaning, so that it is not clear to the listener. Thirdly the speaker may generalise about something without considering particular relevant cases and of course "all generalizations are wrong".

NLP contains a framework called the Meta Model, for unravelling these deletions, distortions and generalizations of language. Anyone who communicates via language will have a full representation of what he means to say. This is called the deep structure and is the fullest possible verbal expression of the idea. The actual language used, however, will delete, distort and generalize this deep structure into a surface structure. We have to do this or all verbal communication would be incredibly long-winded and pedantic. In teaching and other situations where clarity is important a fuller version than the usual shorthand way of expression (the surface structure) may be needed.

There are twelve main ways that language can be ambiguous and there are corresponding Meta Model questions to clarify what has been said and recover unspoken facts and assumptions that need to come out into the open. This is not in any way an exhaustive survey of the Meta Model. There is a good introduction to it in Magic Demystified by B. Lewis and F. Pucelik (1982). It is dealt with in great detail in the Structure of Magic 1 (1975), by John Grinder and Richard Bandler.

Meta Model questions help in three ways. Firstly they gather information. They are precise ways for teachers to get facts and experiences from their students. The questions will connect the language used to the primary sensory experience that gave rise to it, for they demand sensory-based answers and not justifications. Secondly, they expand limits. Students will make statements and ask questions that indicate they believe themselves to be more limited than they really are. "I can't do this!" is the classic example of such a limiting statement. Thirdly, the questions can show exactly what a student means and clear up any misunderstandings between what he means and what a teacher thinks he means.

A word of warning. It is not appropriate to analyse pedantically what a student (or anybody) says in all its minutiae. It rapidly annoys people if used indiscriminately. These questions are a useful systematic approach to clearer communication where necessary and appropriate, and should only be used where there is already good rapport and you are working together towards an agreed outcome.

1)*Unspecified Verb*

A description of how something was done may not be specific enough. A student may say "I played really badly". This is a vague statement and could have many meanings. It could be a plea for encouragement, it could be asking indirectly for praise. It could be a statement of the truth as the student sees it, or he could be reading your mind and forestalling what he thinks you are going to say by saying it himself first. It is impossible to know the reason he might have said it just from the words. A teacher might make a reasonable guess from what he knows about the student, but one of the advantages of the Meta Model is that it makes guessing unnecessary. Guessing is trying to fill in someone else's meaning from your own experience. The Meta Model is not directly concerned with finding out why a person said something, although this will often become clear in the process. The Meta Model is about gathering information, giving choices and clarifying meanings.

"I played really badly" is not a very useful statement because there is too much missing from the verb "to play". He has not been specific about how he plays badly and if anything is going to change, this must be recovered by asking "How do you play badly?"

"What do you play badly?"

"When do you play badly?"

What the teacher needs is an accurate description of what, when, where and particularly how the student thinks he plays badly. These questions are a precise and systematic way of asking "What do you mean?" The best musical example of an unspecified verb is probably:

"Go and practise that for next week"

2)*Comparatives*

These are self-explanatory. If one thing is to be compared with another then both must be mentioned. The key words here are "good", "bad", "better", "worse". The last sentence: "I played really badly" is· also an example of a comparison, something cannot be bad unless it is compared with something that is better (or worse). A comparison must be between two things and one has been deleted here. So the question to ask is "badly compared with what?"

It makes a difference whether the comparison is with the teacher, a world class virtuoso, their friend who has started at the same time, or what they themselves did last week. Sometimes a student makes unfair comparisons, for example by measuring his progress against another student who is studying a different instrument.

Students tend to use comparatives a great deal, nearly always to their own disadvantage. The unspoken standard of comparison is often an ideal, or the teacher's skill level; the product of many years playing experience. One excellent way to make yourself depressed about your own playing is to select an unrealistically high standard of comparison, and measure how far you fall short of it. If you then delete the standard, all you are left with is the bad feeling and no practical steps to take to combat it.

Another example might be:

"Carulli was a poor composer"

(Compared with whom? Beethoven?)

3)*Lost Performatives*

Here a judgement has been made, but the person who has made the judgement is missing. The criteria for making the judgement are often missing as well. Lost performatives are closely allied to comparatives, but the judgement need not involve a comparison. One example which music teachers may hear is the student who says he cannot sing. Often this idea comes from experiences in school music lessons, where the student has been told so directly, or it had been implied. Could the teacher who said this be wrong? How long ago was this?

Judgements may be perfectly reasonable but sometimes it is necessary to know who has made them and on what grounds.

So the questions to ask are:

"Who says?"

"How do you know?"

Students may have unrealistic standards of how good they think they should be, derived from a shadowy authority figure.

Another example would be:

"The guitar is considered to be a hard instrument."

"Who specifically thinks this?" is the question to ask.

4) *Unspecified Referential Index*

The person or thing acting, or being acted on by a verb is called the referential index, so a noun phrase needs clarification if it does not specifically say to what its verb refers. The referential index may be deleted completely. For example "It was taught." The teacher is missing completely. Thinking in the passive voice can make you feel helpless, there is no active subject.

The referential index can be present but unspecified. For example "They taught it" (Who specifically taught it?), or it can be generalized, eg. "Teachers taught it". (Which teacher specifically?) Each is a little more specific and all may be adequate in particular circumstances.

Examples are:

"Teachers work hard"

"Students are undisciplined"

Another example is: "Music is hard"

"Which music?" would be a good reply, or "What specific piece do you find hard?"

5) *Generalizations*

The last example; "Music is hard" is also an example of a generalization. These linguistic categories will often overlap, the vaguer the statement.The more Meta Model violations there will be and the more the categories will overlap.

A generalization is when a whole diverse category of experience is limited by one particular label. In the example above, the speaker is extending his limited experience of music to cover all music. "Music is hard" is a very limiting belief and is liable to act as a self-fulfilling prophecy.

Generalizations can be challenged by bringing their absurdity into focus by exaggeration. So if someone says "The guitar is generally considered to be a difficult instrument", you could reply "Every single person says the guitar is a hard instrument?" Exceptions can easily be cited as well: "I know someone who thinks the guitar is very easy."

One form of generalization is known as complex equivalence. This is when two experiences are linked together; one is taken as the equivalent of the other. For example "You cannot be a good teacher unless you have trained at music college" is a complex equivalence. "Good teacher" is being made equivalent to a college training, but the evidence for this belief is missing and it is presented as being true in every case.

A complex equivalence is challenged by finding an exception: "Have you ever known a good teacher who did not go to music college?", or better "How do you know?" The connection between the two subjects has to be questioned.

6)*Universal Quantifiers*

These are closely allied to generalizations, and are words like "all", "every", "no-one", "always". Examples that I have heard in lessons are "I always play that wrong", and "I'll never be able to play that piece".

These sorts of phrases may be requests for encouragement, but it is no use simply asserting the opposite "Oh, yes, you will be able to". Clarification is needed. One way to challenge a universal quantifier is to exaggerate and say: "What, you'll never, ever, ever be able to do it under any circumstances?" or "Has there never been a time when you played it correctly?" Even better in this case might be "How do you know?"

Sometimes I totally agree with and exaggerate the statement by saying "You're right. You'll never be able to play that piece, why not give up now? It's quite hopeless." This will usually get a rapid reply on the lines of "Well hold on, I might. I won't give up yet."

7)Nominalization

A nominalization is a verb or process that has been turned into a noun and is very characteristic of the digital representational system. Education, teaching and learning are all examples of very useful nominalizations and I use them liberally in this book. If a noun is not sensory-based, if it cannot be seen and touched, it is a nominalization and likely to have maximum ambiguity. It needs to be made into a verb and put back into the process from which it came originally. Nominalizations are really verbs masquerading as nouns, and by definition delete the referential index.

"Who is educating whom about what?"

"Who is learning from whom and what are they learning?"

"How and when are they learning it?"

'Practice' is a favourite nominalization, it deserves, and will have a section to itself later. Suffice to say for the moment, unless when, what, and especially how to practise is specified, it is a word that is much too vague to be much use in a music lesson.

Memory is another nominalization. "I've got a bad memory" is a statement that can be challenged on several fronts.

"Bad in relation to what?"

"What do you have trouble memorizing?"

"How do you memorize?"

With answers to these questions, specific problems can be pinpointed and then actually solved.

A process frozen into a noun has lost the possibility for changing and developing. You are stuck if you believe you have a bad memory, but you can change if you think about how you memorize. A process can unfold, but a noun is static. A person who thinks in nominalizations is liable to feel helpless and passive.

Technique is a very useful shorthand word for a very complex physical and mental process. At times, it will need to be analysed into its elements.

Many nominalizations have thousands of books

written about them. This book is an attempt to denominalize 'Teaching' and 'Learning', and provide a useful working model for understanding them.

8)*Modal Operators of Possibility*
Many of these linguistic patterns show the limits of what students think they can do, so it is good to challenge them. Modal operators of possibility are words like "can", and "cannot", "possible" and "impossible". They define, in the speaker's judgement, what is possible or not. The limiting ones "cannot" and "impossible" need to be challenged. A student who says "I can play this scale" has no problem (unless he constantly makes a complete mess of it, then his idea of the ability to play a scale needs to be questioned). A student who says "I can't play this scale" is limited. Teachers work mainly to break down these limitations and the first step is to challenge the modal operators.

The question to ask is "What stops you?" Often it is not a student's ability, but his belief that stops him. At the very least it will pinpoint a technical difficulty. Whatever the reason, a teacher needs precise information.

A student may say to me "I can't play this piece". In reply, I would ask which particular part of the piece, or when does it go wrong. It cannot all go wrong simultaneously, we have to start somewhere. "All of it" is not an acceptable answer. First we must narrow down to a particular section, even if that is the very first bar. I can then ask "What prevents you from playing it?" or "What exactly goes wrong when you play this section?"

A good approach is "Show me how you play it wrongly". If a student knows he is doing it wrong, he must have some hazy idea about what it would sound like if it was right. He may not know exactly what he is doing wrong, but we do have common ground on which to start working. Sometimes he knows exactly what he is doing wrong, but leaves it to me, the teacher, to correct it because that is supposed to be my job. He may tell me that a chord change is always too slow, or a left hand finger is too weak to sound a note. In the end, it must come down to some specific difficulty with timing, reading or finding the notes, then we can work on a specific remedy.

Another sentence I often hear is "I can't relax my hand". Again there must be some representation of what it would be like if it were relaxed, so I ask "How would you know if it was relaxed?" "Relax" is an unspecified verb, so the student's idea of relaxation must be obtained first. I can do this by asking her to imagine a time when she was relaxed and to describe it to me. Her idea may not be the same as mine. When I know what "relaxing" means to her, I can compare it with my own idea and see what she is actually doing.

Also, in order to describe her feeling of relaxation to me, she will actually have to relax. If I notice her body language, I will be able to see in future when she is relaxed, because I will know what to look for.

When anyone says that he cannot do something, he must also know what it would be like if he could. We can take this as the positive goal and see what is preventing it being realised; this is better than concentrating on the negative side. The best way to walk a dead straight line is to look ahead to where you want to go and aim for that. Looking at your feet to try to line them up straight almost guarantees an uncertain path.

9)*Modal Operators of Necessity*

These are "should", "shouldn't","must" and "mustn't". There is an unspoken rule of conduct operating. The words imply that it is necessary that something does or does not happen, so you need to find out the imagined consequences. Thus the response. to a statement that contains "shouldn't" or "mustn't" is "What would happen if you did?". For example: "You shouldn't let your left hand finger joints collapse when playing". By asking "what would happen if you did?" the various technical reasons can be discussed and evaluated.

The challenge to "should" and "must" is "What would happen if you did not do that?" It is important to get the other side of the rule, the consequences if it were not followed. "I should do more practice" is answered by "What would happen if you did not?" All these linguistic usages can be analysed from both a teacher's and a student's point of view.

"Should" is a word of many facets. As a modal operator, the consequences may be very clear, for example "You shouldn't drink and drive". However it can be used very loosely indeed. It tends to accompany lost performatives (judgements) and gains a moral aspect which it usually does not deserve. It is also often interpreted as a command, especially in an example like "You should practise more".

If I tell a student "You should be able to play this scale", I am really stating my belief that he is capable of doing so at this particular time. This may or may not be a reasonable assumption. It is much easier to deal with modal operators of possibility than modal operators of necessity, and only to talk about what a student can or cannot do in the here and now. This does not preclude helping him to become more skilful.

"Should" is often interpreted as a rebuke and I think the word is best left out of a lesson. Young students often feel that they are being told off for not doing something that they "ought" to be able to do then and there, and an idea of failure is introduced. It does not matter whether that is what the teacher intends, if that is how the student understands it at the time, then that is what it means.

Students will often say they "should" be able to do something and they may not have good grounds for this judgement. Some of my adult students, especially if they play another instrument, feel they "should" therefore be able to progress quickly and easily on the guitar, but that does not follow at all. "Should" can easily become a word that evokes instant guilt about the gap between expectation and reality. The question is, are the expectations realistic? Are they helpful? Saying "You should be able to do this" is often a blaming, angry response from someone who is not directly admitting his anger or his expectations. He may be annoyed at his own inability to communicate. I banish modal operators of necessity from all my lessons.

There are three further patterns that underlie and influence our communication and cause misunderstandings. These are presuppositions, mind reading and causal modelling. They are all ultimately. due to a mismatch between two different models of the world.

Presuppositions

Behind all the language we use, there are unspoken ideas we take for granted. We all make assumptions that stem from our basic beliefs, but on a personal, circumstantial level, some assumptions may be mistaken and need to be questioned. For example, just because a student has done an examination that involves some theory of harmony, it does not follow that he knows what a subdominant is. He "should", but he may not.

If I tell a student "You must do more practice", the assumption is that he does not do enough, although this is not stated explicitly. If I say "When you have finished playing this piece we will discuss your mistakes", I am presupposing he will play it to the end and will make some errors. In fact I have really given him a direct command to make errors, for it supplies him with a reason for playing the music in the first place. This is a rather blatant example, but teachers can sometimes phrase their instructions in such a way as to assume the student will slip up. On a covert level, it is surprising how many teachers and students unconsciously take this phrase as a model of the structure of any lesson.

While there are presuppositions behind why a student comes to a lesson in the first place, the important point is whether these assumptions are limiting or not. If teachers and students make assumptions (and we certainly have to make some), they may as well be positive ones that do not restrict the possibilities before they have even been explored.

Some examples of unhelpful presuppositions (with other Meta Model ambiguities) are:

"Why is your timing so bad?"

"Can you play that again without the wrong notes?"

"When you practise more, you'll be able to play this."

Causal Modelling

Causal modelling means using the unspecified verbs "cause" or "make" to link some external happening to a subjective response, when it is not clear how the two are connected. For example "Hearing that piece makes me angry", or "Using a footstool makes me feel uncomfortable". Also there are statements like "I did not have time to practise last week because my goldfish died".

The best response is to ask how specifically one thing causes the other. As I said earlier, cause and effect are built into the English language to a large extent and this implies being helpless and at the whim of external events. Sometimes the student may feel he must make some excuse about why he has not touched the instrument from one week's end to the other which he may not even take seriously himself.

Students often feel and may be encouraged to feel that a teacher's demands are right and proper and must be met. If for some reason they cannot, then they are at fault and some excuse is required to absolve them from blame. Barring unconsciousness for a week, I cannot think of any reason why students cannot find a few minutes to play every day, and often that is all that is required. If they protest they cannot and say they are put upon by external forces outside their control (and they may well view the teacher as one of these), I try to explain that it is a question of choice. It was not that they could not, but that they chose not to. There may be perfectly good reasons for that choice which I must respect. Responsibility and choice work both ways. Next week they may choose to find the time. Blame and guilt are irrelevant and dis-tracting. Choice gives freedom. Cause and effect imply helplessness.

One unpleasant by-product of thinking in terms of cause and effect is that you can give people the power to create feelings in you, over which you have no control. No-one can actually force another to feel an emotion, it is a matter of choice; choose the pleasant feeling, reject the unpleasant. A teacher may say "That student just makes me lose my temper!" Really there is no forced connection. I do not believe that anyone can compel another person into any state of mind by their body language or by what they say. The mirror image of this belief in cause and effect is to shoulder an unreasonable resonsibility for what other people feel, because you think you have caused it, and therefore bear some responsibility. You must therefore take extreme care over what you say and do. You become either the victim or the nursemaid of others. One prevalent cause-effect belief in education is that teaching causes learning. This certainly does not follow.

Mind Reading

Mind reading is a form of presupposition where one person assumes he knows what another person is thinking. It often involves attributing one's own reaction to another person; for example the visual person who assumes you are not listening if you are not looking at him.

When someone says to me "I don't know how you can listen to the same pieces badly played all the time, it must be awful", he is mind reading (and violating most of the other Meta Model categories as well!). Very seldom is there enough sensory-based evidence to enable someone to attribute an opinion or feeling to another person.

Mind reading is challenged by asking "How do you know?" This is a better response than "Why do you say that?", which usually results in justifications rather than observations. I remember one good example of mind reading by a student who was playing a difficult piece by

Francisco Tarrega. While I was listening, I propped my forehead in my left hand and rested my left elbow on the arm of my chair. When he had finished playing, we talked about the piece. He was defensive and said he knew I thought he was playing very badly. When I asked him how he knew, he told me that he assumed my posture to be one of weary despair, whereas it actually had no significance whatsoever.

I have outlined briefly some of the ways that we can clarify what is said in a lesson, to gain useful information, and identify the limits of what students think they can do. They can be guided past these limits.

These twelve linguistic patterns are only generalizations themselves and must always be applied in a particular context. The meaning of what someone says can also be radically transformed by his body language, voice tonality and facial expression. Some patterns are more important than others. When a student says "That always goes wrong!", the generalization is the least important. It may be that every time he has played that piece it has actually gone wrong. The first thing to do is to find out what it is that goes wrong, and secondly how specifically it goes wrong. (The unspecified noun and the unspecified verb). In my own teaching I nearly always challenge lost performatives (judgements), comparatives and both types of modal operator.

I use these Meta Model questions when I am trying to find out exactly how a student plays, if he makes a mistake by misreading a note, or by missing a fret, I want to know exactly how he does it. I want specific instructions so that I could do it too, then we will both understand much better and find a way to correct it. I also use these questions systematically to discover what successful learners do and what strategies they use. This is called modelling a skill. By finding out exactly how very good musicians play, their successful strategies can be taught to everyone.

Guitar technique on the physical, visible level, is a model of what good guitarists do to play well, but there is tremendous scope for modelling the internal processes they use to learn, as well as the external techniques they use to play so well.

Sometimes, however, I want to be as imprecise as possible, to ensure a student interprets my instructions in his own way, bringing his own resources to bear on phrasing, interpretation and emotional feeling in a piece of music. I deliberately violate as many of these Meta Model categories as I can, to be as vague as possible. I talk of understandings, feelings, pictures, learning and responses, and the student has to interpret these words in his own terms. I choose not to impose my own content. This gives him maximum freedom to use his own ideas.

Chapter Three

The Two Sides of the Brain

All our sense impressions are sorted, filtered and interpreted by the brain and our learning and powers of memory are dependent on it organizing and storing the sensory information.

The cerebrum is the largest and most evolved part of the brain and is divided into two halves which are connected by tissue known as the corpus callosum. The left side of the brain controls and receives sensations from the right side of the body. The right side of the brain controls and receives sensations from the left side of the body. This nervous organization is known as contralateral, which means literally 'opposite-sided'.

Experiments which have measured the electrical activity in both hemispheres for different tasks have shown that they have different but complementary functions.

It has been found that damage to the left brain hemisphere nearly always interferes with, or even totally destroys a person's language ability. Damage to the right hemisphere does not do this, but badly disturbs bodily awareness (kinaesthetic sense), musical ability and spatial awareness. Speech and language are intimately linked with thinking and reasoning, and so the left side was named the dominant, the right, the minor hemisphere.

This specialisation of the brain hemispheres holds for 98% of the population. Left or right handedness seems to make very little difference, although a small number of left-handed people have these functions in the opposite hemisphere to normal and another small group of left-handed people have them dispersed over both hemispheres.

The two brain hemispheres are like two separate people with specialised tasks. The left deals with language, analysis, and sequencing ability. It solves problems by taking one piece of information after another. It works like an extremely powerful computer and understands by making comparisons.

The right deals with non-verbal and spatial aware-ness, visual imagery, pattern recognition and music ap-preciation. It processes incoming information in a ho-listic way. Normally the corpus callosum allows these two parts of the brain to share information, so that we can make sense of the world. A visual metaphor would be to think of the right side of the brain as an impression-ist painter, the left side as a draughtsman. To create a fine work of art needs both of these skills.

Left Hemisphere	Right Hemisphere
Rational	Intuitive
Digital	Analogic
Language	Non-verbal
Analytical	Holistic
Objective	Subjective

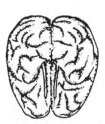

Figure 2

It is important to remember that these are descriptions of the different ways the hemispheres process information and not the type of information they deal with. For example, recent studies have shown the right hemisphere was not so active while reading analytical technical material, but was much more active when the subject was reading stories. Many things happen simultaneously in stories, they do not usually progress in a simple linear way. Language in the form of stories stimulates the right hemisphere. Ideally the two halves of the brain work together to complement each other. An insight without the language to express it cannot be readi-ly shared. On the other hand, linguistic fluency is wasted if there is no overall perspective to develop and elabor-ate creative thought.

When we wish to find out something from another person, we use language and tend to define a person's knowledge and understanding by what he can tell us verbally. This assumption is a mistake, we are aware of very much more than we can verbally articulate.

While sounds and sensations are dealt with contralaterally by the brain, the visual cross-over is more complicated. The left side of retina connects with the left side of the brain, and the right side of each retina connects with the right side of the brain. So when looking straight ahead the left side of the visual field goes to the right side of the brain, and the right side of the visual field to the left hemisphere.

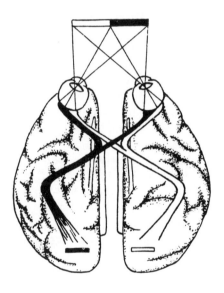

Left Hemisphere   Right Hemisphere

Figure 3

This associates with the eye accessing cues. Eye movement up and to the left tends to access eidetic images in the right hemisphere, for the left visual field is represented there. Eye movement up and to the right, associated with constructed images , will access the left hemisphere.

Visualising a picture involves the right hemisphere and is quite different from 'imagining' a picture. The latter tends to use language to construct the scene and so uses the dominant hemisphere.

Musical Skills

Music is not a single skill or talent which is present or not, but a complex interaction of many different sub-skills, most of which can be used independently in other fields. It is wrong to say musical ability is 'in' the right hemisphere, although crucial parts of it certainly seem to be. Right hemisphere damage nearly always disturbs musical ability, but left hemisphere damage often does too.

Music appreciation involves structural, harmonic and rhythmic analysis, as well as awareness of the total design of a piece. It is possible to marvel at the ingenuity of a composition while not actually liking or being convinced by the overall result.

On a simpler level, a study (T. Beaver and R. Chiarello 1975) showed that subjects who had no musical training in the previous five years were more successful in aural tests when using the left ear rather than the right. These tests involved the recognition of simple melodies. This makes sense; the left ear connects primarily with the right hemisphere.

This finding was reversed for musically experienced listeners. They had greater success when listening solely through the right ear. Beaver and Chiarello explained this by saying that musical sophistication means a greater capacity for musical analysis and appreciating sequences of sound. The aural tests measured the ability to hear and recognise sound sequences and so would use the dominant hemisphere to a greater extent. Earphones were used in these tests, so the music went to one or the other ear exclusively. In normal situations of course music will be heard by both ears, regardless of which way we face. People who do well in musical aptitude tests also tend to do better in language tests and other left hemisphere skills; so the picture is not clear.

Music learning involves a combination of left and right brain skills. Sometimes concentration on the visual-spatial aspects of music is more useful than a verbal explanation. I often find myself explaining leger lines, working out that:

is an E and relating it to the notes on the stave which are already familiar. Sometimes I think my students have understood the idea until I ask them to draw notes with leger lines. They will then draw examples that look like this:

or:

I deal with this by turning the stave on its side and telling them to ignore what it means but just to treat it as a pattern. It is easy then to add lines and keep going across.

Sometimes we try so hard to understand the abstract meaning, it clouds the simple visual perception. Most music teaching concentrates on abstract memory and verbal explanation, it misses the visual pattern. Reading music involves recognising patterns and often concentrating on this aspect instead of using words can be very successful.

Memory

Memory can be usefully divided into recognition and recall. Recognition is when we meet an idea, sight, sound, smell, taste or touch that we know we have encountered before. It is familiar, although it may not have entered our mind for years. Sense impressions leave memory traces and we are forever matching, sorting and recognizing new sensory input in terms of what we know already. Stopping at simple recognition will put an end to curiosity, further investigation and possible new discovery.

Recall is the ability to recreate some idea, sight, sound, smell, taste or touch; to draw it from memory. If I play the notes d, f, a and ask a student to identify the chord, he would (I hope) say it was a minor chord. He would not be able to say it was a chord of D minor unless he had perfect pitch, or knew what notes I was playing and knew enough music theory to deduce the answer. He would recognise it as a minor chord by matching it successfully with his internal auditory representation of a minor chord. Building up reliable internal auditory representations which can be recalled at will, is the purpose of aural training.

He could probably be able to sing it back to me a few moments later by recalling it from memory. But if I waited longer it is unlikely that he could recall it well enough to sing it back (at pitch) even if I bribed him outrageously. Powers of recall are more limited than powers of recognition, but they can be helped by using more than one internal sense and by frequent repetition and backup. Anything is very difficult to remember using only one sense, in this case it is auditory. The more internal senses brought into action, the easier the recall.

Memory is to do with the retention of information in the broadest sense, so that it is available, but not necessarily conscious, at any one time. It may need to be triggered by some association. There is quite good evidence that everything leaves a memory trace, but some things are more accessible to the conscious mind than others. Understanding is the ability to make connections between new facts and previous knowledge and experience. Learning involves a possible change in response, it is the ability for purposeful modification of action.

Short-term Memory

Memory is the first step in the chain of learning a skill. Defining the difference between short-term and long-term memory is rather like asking how long is a piece of string. Generally speaking, short-term memory will retain facts which have not been reviewed and consolidated. Once they have, they will pass into long-term memory, but this definition is not rigid. Some things are "once seen, never forgotten"; so impressive they are effortlessly memorable, so the strength of the initial stimulus is important too.

Anything you wish to remember needs to be given attention in the here and now, the senses need to be directed outwardly and not inwardly. The more senses that are brought into play, the better the memory, and the more association and references there will be to what is already known. Anything that is interesting, relevant and meaningful will catch our attention and hold it. The appeal it has for us will depend on our personal experience and state of mind at the time.

There are some useful facts about short and long-term memory that can help teachers present their lessons more effectively. Research has shown that facts are best remembered when they occur in the first or last few minutes of a lesson. This is when the most important points can be put over. We are least likely to recall anything that is said about three-quarters of the way through the lesson. We are also obviously most likely to recall anything that seems unusual or strange. It is "out of the ordinary", and our mind remembers difference, not similarity. It is worth putting points across in imaginative or bizarre ways. For example to tell a student to be as lazy as possible in her guitar playing is more memorable than telling her to make the minimum movements necessary. So such things as underlining notes in purple, making puns and telling stories to illustrate musical facts do help memory. And they add interest and fun to the lesson.

Seven Plus or Minus Two

Our minds can only handle a limited amount of information at any one time. Our short-term memory is limited to about seven discrete facts or 'chunks'. This 'Law of seven plus or minus two' was first put forward by George Miller in the *American Psychologist* in 1956.

A 'chunk' in this context is a pattern of information that is not yet familiar enough to be unconscious or known automatically, so it must be consciously remembered. The size of the chunk is variable, it is dependent on the learner's prior knowledge. These patterns will be small at the beginning of any instrumental learning, but when they are assimilated and learned, they become unconscious, and the mind is free to attend to larger patterns. These larger patterns may be composed of a series of already known smaller patterns, or they may be completely new. In the first lesson, a chunk would be a single note. Years later, a chunk might be a harmonic progression, or several chords.

The ability to remember music at any level will depend on seeing the overall principles so large 'chunks' can be assimilated. For example:

It would be very difficult to remember this as a series of disconnected notes. There are far too many chunks to carry in short-term memory, yet a competent musician could probably play it on his instrument after studying it

for a few moments. He would remember the key, the
time signature and the sequence of scales. He would also
notice the harmony; tonic, subdominant, dominant, end-
ing on a perfect cadence. The music has been 'chunked'
at a high level. The musician's ability to organise on a
high level like this has been built up by his training, he
sees a certain group of connections. The whole tune is
quite regular and predictable in these terms.

Contrast the last example with this tune:

This is much harder to remember. Its profile is not so
regular, although it shares certain features with the last
example. It cannot be organized into large 'chunks' easily.

Here is a non-musical example:

2764125216343

This would take some effort to memorise unless you
see that it is patterned by a principle that springs from the
numbers themselves. It is each number in turn from 3
to 7 cubed.

Without seeing this, the next best way to remember it
would be to break it down by some device such as jug-
gling with familiar telephone numbers or street numbers
that might fit. These sort of memory aids are called mnemonics. Least effective and taking the most effort would
be to repeat it over and over again until it was
'chunked' in memory as one unit. Then you remember it
completely, or not at all. Some music memorization is
like this if you can only start a piece from the beginning.

Memory overlaps with understanding, which is the
connection of new material with existing knowledge.
The more we can organise our material into meaningful
groups or patterns, the more facts we can take in. Good

memory and understanding is a function of being able to organise, sequence, and connect patterns of information. The desperate 'swotting' over textbooks just does not work, it is almost impossible to remember information without organising and connecting it in some meaningful way. If it is not organically organised, then it will have to be linked in other ways. Organization depends on the ability to see patterns that spring from the material itself. These are likely to be the same ones the composer has used, consciously or unconsciously.

One of the secrets of good teaching is the ability to organise and sequence chunks for each individual learner; this makes progress smooth and easy. Overload in either number or complexity of the chunks results in difficulty and frustration. However naturally a student takes to the instrument at the beginning, it is worth resisting the temptation to add new topics.

The teacher will have the whole of his conscious attention, that is, his seven plus or minus two capacity to devote to the student's playing. The student is not in such a good position to monitor his own playing, for he rarely has any spare capacity, his mind is fully taken up in organising and performing the complex movements needed to play the instrument. The most important thing a teacher can give his student is attention.

Sequence

A teacher must make a skills analysis of instrumental playing. This means breaking down musical knowledge and necessary playing skills into their component parts. However, teaching is not simply passing these on in a reasonable sequence. Would that it were. The order in which they are passed on will be different for each student, because each student brings his own different perceptions, strategies and personality to the lesson.

Students need particular skills to play the guitar and knowledge of how to read music, which will be built up in a logical way from the nature of the task and the work we do together. I do not feel I have to impose any predetermined sequence which would override this process. The student will show me what he needs to do and I must give attention to see it and work on it. I will know in a general way what the student can do already and in what direction he is going.

So although teachers may know more facts and have more experience than their students, they cannot know what is best for them at any time. The best teaching sequence is built from a skills analysis of music and the instrument, tempered by the student's perceived and expressed needs at any time.

Teaching is often seen as presenting information in a predetermined sequence, with a schedule of rewards and punishments. There is constant time pressure to cover syllabuses and this can stifle a student's natural learning process. Time pressure is one of the most destructive enemies of learning. Music is a formal structure, and can be manipulated in a formal way. It is easy, but misleading to think that it must therefore be taught or communicated in a formal way. The content of a message does not determine the way in which it is passed on.

Acquiring a skill such as guitar playing can be seen as learning small skills which become so familiar that they do not need to be thought about, and building them up continuously into more complicated skills. Larger chunks are built up by the student connecting up the smaller ones, and these links will be made in his own way.

Our knowledge builds up by making connections, not by simple addition. It is like building a wall, bricks have to be cemented together for the wall to stand, not just piled one on top of the other. The cement is just as important as the bricks. Facts have a different meaning, that is, a different set of connections, for different people. We cannot expect a student to understand something in the same way we do, for although we may give him the information, we cannot give him our connections.

Mnemonics

One way of linking facts to help memory is by using mnemonics. The word comes from the Greek mneme, which means to remember. A mnemonic is any technique that helps people to remember things. It can be a rhyme, a visual image, an acrostic, or a chiming digital watch. It works by establishing an association between two things hitherto unconnected. This association works best if it is simple and unique, even exaggerated. Visual imagery is a strong point and a clear picture is a good memory aid.

Mnemonics translate the abstract into the concrete and so make it more memorable. There is evidence that many people remember music better if they give it a title that represents a definite feeling or object. Abstract conceptual titles are less memorable. This would be even more important when teaching children, whose interest is engaged far more by titles that represent something real. "A Walk in the Country" is much more appealing than "Andante Grazioso" There does need to be a basis for these titles in the character of the music.

Acrostics are very useful in music teaching. The notes on the lines of the stave are EGBDF. This is difficult to remember; it has no meaning, "Every Good Boy Deserves Football" is easy. EADGBE (the open strings of a guitar) becomes; "Elephants and Dinosaurs Grow Beards Easily". The odder the mnemonic, the more likely it is to be remembered. We often think that strange things are difficult to work out and remember, but the opposite is true. We remember the odd and strange events in our lives.

The more senses that are involved, the more likely something is to be remembered. This applies to the internal as well as the external use of the senses. For a long time I was puzzled by the fact that although I used mnemonics with students, it seemed to make no difference to how well they remembered. I used the old favourites FACE for the notes in the spaces of the stave, and "Every Good Boy Deserves Football" for the notes on the lines. Often children would volunteer these anyway from previous music lessons (and would then be at a loss for the letter name of a note). When it came to a situation where it could be actually applied, they never did, they forgot, and now I think I know why. Left at an abstract level, mnemonics are not much use. I think they would be stored as language constructions in the left hemisphere. However, if I ask the students to make a picture of a FACE for example, and make it as bizarre as possible, then this is much more memorable. If I then ask them to make the face say "face in the space", and to hear that internally, then to imagine the feeling this would invoke, the results are best of all. To be most effective, mnemonics have to be filled out by the internal senses.

There is evidence that mnemonics utilise the right hemisphere, whereas the usual verbal learning techniques involve only the left hemisphere ('Analysis of a Mnemonic Device Gordon Bower, *American Scientist* 58:504). When the left side of the brain has been damaged, some memory powers are lost. Mnemonics have helped people with such damage to improve their memory by using the unharmed right side.

Strong visual imagery is another right brain function that helps association and memory. This is true for both strong and weak visualisers. For example I have found that children may become mixed up between 1,2,3,4, representing left hand fingers, and numbers in a circle standing for the strings. Given a vivid visual image of a string in a ring (which can be different for each child) coupled with the imagined sound of the string, and the feeling of striking the string, this need not be a problem.

Eidetic Memory

Everybody has an almost perfect photographic memory, but it lasts for only one tenth of a second. It is the basis for the store of remembered images in the internal visual sense. However, some people have it developed to a higher degree, and can hold the image in their mind for much longer. This persisting eidetic imagery is like a controlled hallucination. There are players who can conjure up a mental picture of the music in their mind and play it by reading from their internal image.

Studies show that 50% of children have the ability for strong eidetic imagery, but nearly all lose it by the age of 14 when its incidence in the general population is about 2%, with only one person in a million showing this talent very strongly. Strong visual imagery is a right brain function, and like any faculty not used regularly, begins to weaken. Without the ability to read, visual memory is much more important. Our schooling with its emphasis on linear ways of understanding "educates" away our visual memory.

The brain hemispheres are not specialised in infants, but functional lateralisation is more or less complete by the age of ten. This may account for the loss of visualising power in older children and adults. As we mature, we use symbolic language more and the right brain less.

It is also possible to have an eidetic auditory sense; perfect pitch is an example of this. People with perfect pitch can give an exact letter name to any note they hear. This talent usually manifests in childhood and is never lost. The incidence of perfect pitch in the general adult population is 2%, the same as for strong eidetic imagery, or 'photographic memory'. There is a much greater chance of having perfect pitch if you start an instrument before the age of five.

Most people can develop a limited sense of perfect pitch, but naturally have only a relative sense of pitch, that is, they can only identify notes in relation to other known ones. They name notes not in isolation, but by comparing the interval between them. Musicians need a better than average auditory memory, and senses can be strengthened with use (or weakened through disuse).

Some of the most famous memory men, those who have shown astounding ability to remember random, meaningless, disconnected lists of objects, have done it by strong associations using eidetic imagery. Sometimes this is accompanied by a degree of synesthesia. This means the senses merge into each other, so that images evoke sounds and feelings, even tastes and smells. They are using the full range of their representational systems. With such strong connected sensual and associative links it is not surprising that these men could recall things so well.

Even with normal people musical notes can evoke a colour or feeling. There is certainly a long history of certain keys in music being associated with certain colours, and whole systems have been built up connecting the two. As both sound and colours are vibrations of a particular frequency, a number of composers have thought there was a significant link between the two.

Reminiscence and Review

In any learning situation it is possible to pass the limit of what can be remembered however well the material is organised. We will have had our seven chunks, in which case it is pointless to carry on.

Instrumental playing time is best broken down into quite small periods, each of 15 to 45 minutes, with a break of 5 to 10 minutes between them. Quite apart from the limitations of our short-term memory, taking a break makes the most of the fact that we best remember beginnings and endings of sessions. Taking three half hour periods we get six such instances instead of the two obtained from one continuous session, when we might be too tired to make the most of the last one anyway.

After a few minutes break we actually recall the material better than at any other time, this is called the reminiscence effect. By reviewing during the break what we did in the previous session, we will get maximum benefit from this way of working.

Work needs to be consolidated for it to pass into long-term memory and so be available if needed. We have to review music or facts we wish to remember. This only needs a few minutes and is best done about 10 minutes after the original work, to make the most of the reminiscence effect. After that, reviewing a few times over the next two days will strengthen the memory.

This continuous reinforcement works, whereas an all-out marathon frontal assault does not. Because the rate of forgetting is highest in the early stages it underlines again the need to play every day, even for a short time, and not try to make up by playing long hours at weekends.

We can make the most of this in very practical terms in the way we learn, and suggest our students learn a piece of music. I often find I try to do too much at once and students fall into this trap too. They will come for their lesson having attempted far too much of the music they are studying; very little of the piece will be coherent and continuous. They may have tried to cover it all every night, and so never really conquered any of it.

A better idea is to work on a small section the first day, and to review it afterwards. The following day take the same section and work at it a little more (consolidation). If it goes well, then go on to another small section and do the same thing. There is a good chance of covering most of the piece by the end of the week and what is more, it will be secure. Even if very little has been done in this way, it is far more valuable than trying to do the whole piece without sufficient attention. Taking a little at a time and continuously consolidating is bound to achieve lasting results. Trying to do too much at once will only result in musical indigestion. What matters is the long term view and how to go about a task. It is more important to tell a student how to play, than what to play.

Long-term Memory

Long-term memory is not an empty bin that gradually gets filled up. Memory is distributed throughout the brain and not localised in discrete sites. After brain damage, intensity of recall is dependent on the amount of brain functioning, but memory overall is remarkably resistant to damage. You can only damage memory by removing parts of the brain (at least in rats), you cannot destroy it.

It is good to memorise only useful information, but there is no danger of ever running out of memory space. As the brain remembers by using and making connections and associations, its storage capacity is analogous to that of a hologram (Karl Pribram 1971). It can probably store a quadrillion items of information (1 followed by 15 noughts). Even 10% of this would be enough to record a hundred bits a second over a lifespan of 75 years! More than enough for anybody. Memory is a growing chain of connections linked by meaning.

Forgetting

Forgetting means that the information in the short-term memory has not been transferred and stored in the long-term memory. It is different from faulty recall, where something is inaccurately remembered. There are many reasons why we forget. Language forces me to describe forgetting as a positive act, but it is not something that can be done willingly, but something that just happens depending on the circumstances. Things we try to forget are usually annoyingly persistent.The more you deliberately try to forget something the more attention you give it, and so the more likely you are to remember it. It is rather like trying to go to sleep, the more you try, the more sleep will elude you.

Forgetting happens easily if the necessary time and attention have not been given in the first place. We need not forget anything if we do not want to, providing we understand how to form clear memories, and back them up at suitable intervals. This has tremendous implications. Forgetting is something we can choose not to do.

Memories decay naturally, if they are not consolidated. How quickly they do so depends on the strength of the initial impression. Sometimes similar memories will merge with, or replace others. This happens for example if we learn a piece of music similar to one we know already. Suddenly we may find that the first piece has been confused with similar sections of the new piece or vice versa. Each piece needs careful attention given to these specific places.

Students may forget things. They may forget particular points you have mentioned in a lesson, often for straightforward reasons, eg. these points may have come three-quarters of the way through the lesson. Important points need to be written down as a visual reminder (especially with strongly visual students).

There is the example of a student who 'accidentally' leaves his music on your music stand when he leaves, so he cannot play it during the week, (and it is not his fault?). He was clearly not keen about the piece in the first place.

I think a student who consistently forgets to bring his or her music to the lesson can be particularly annoying. This ploy can reduce a teacher to a nervous wreck in a few weeks. If a student consistently forgets his music, he may be making a non-verbal statement about the lessons or the teaching, but this is difficult to find out directly. If you can find some way to jog his memory, at least then he will have a conscious choice about whether he brings his music or not.

When students keep forgetting their music, I usually tell them to make sure they forget it again next week. This is a good idea from at least two points of view. Firstly it is odd enough to be memorable, and secondly the more they try to obey you, the less they are able to.

One week I tried this trick on two girls after they had persistently forgotten their music. The next week they came back and said they had obeyed instructions! They had forgotten. When I asked if it had come to mind at all, each said yes, but only after she had gone to bed the night before the lesson. I asked them again to try and forget the music, but if they remembered at any time the night before, to put it in their case immediately. They agreed. Then I said "For heaven's sake don't remember it after you've gone to bed, or you will have to get up again to put it in your case!" They were not able to forget after that and have brought it ever since.

Education and the Right Brain

The analytical methods based on the left brain use of language, will mostly take care of themselves. Education favours the left brain, and inadequate education in its own terms leads to inadequate verbal and linguistic skills. Inadequate right brain training has bad effects too and most of these occur in the arts. Opposing theories can both be convincing from a purely rational standpoint. While both may hold together logically, what is needed is an overview of both, a dialectical approach to find a third way that takes the contradictions into account, and this is exactly what the right brain can supply. Great art and scientific discovery shows this same principle at work.

If the left brain tries to take over the right brain functions, there is a sense of trying to measure the drops of water in a river flowing past, counting the number of angels on the head of a pin, or trying to find the beauty of a butterfly by pulling it to pieces: complicated, confusing and ultimately impossible. To try to make the right brain work like the left brain gives magic, where naming something gives you control of it, where parts are the same as wholes and ends and means lose their connection as part of the same process. Both these ways of thinking are quite prevalent in our culture.

It seems to me that modern education is overbalanced towards the left brain to an unhealthy extent, not only in content but more crucially, in method. Sequenced teaching, time schedules, seats in rows, and especially grades all show this. While it is good to develop the analytical and language skills to the full, it need not be at the expense of the more artistic right brain functions. Left brain rational analytical thinking dominates our culture and is highly valued. Intuitive thinking, making leaps by seeing unusual connections is given little opportunity.

Some widely-used educational approaches are not very effective, they may have become established before we had gained more sophisticated psychological and physiological information. There are many studies to show that people using visual imagery and association could remember about three times better than people using rote repetition with a list of words (Ralph Haber 1970). Rote repetition is tiring, long winded and ineffective. It also relies heavily on the internal auditory sense, so is not appropriate for all students anyway. Such learning uses only a narrow range of faculties, but anything else is often seen as a form of cheating and therefore not mentioned. Most of the evidence suggests that there is nothing actually wrong with so-called under-achievers, they are simply using less effective learning strategies than their 'brighter' contemporaries. Learning strategies do not figure prominently in the curriculum which is most concerned with what should be taught, rather than how learning takes place and how to maximize it. Studies have shown that when everyone was taught to use associative mental imagery, memory differences all but disappeared (A.Buzan 1977). Any form of education that does not teach effective learning strategies, widens, rather than closes, the gap between children with different abilities.

Music notation is an abstract system and very difficult for younger children to understand. Maturity expands our ability to go from the concrete to the abstract with the help of language. Imagery can help younger children particularly by making facts more vivid and concrete; for it uses their stronger powers of visualization. The more teachers can make learning easier for their students this way, the more pleasant lessons will become. So much education seems to be rather like getting children to jump obstacles with their feet tied together (so they can't cheat).

Children who use their artistic powers more than most are often classed as "underachieving", when in fact their ways of learning are just different from those of their fellows. I think our education lacks balance, and we are only half educated. Less than that in fact, because even the left brain is not developed very well. No wonder it is a psychological truism to say most people only use 10% of their possible mental powers. The artistic powers associated with the right brain are neglected; so we try to solve problems in an analytical, logical way, even when this approach is not suitable. Sightreading, drawing and music composition are examples.

It is worth remembering that we all "underachieve". Some people draw badly, some have little talent for music, others have poor physical co-ordination and find sports difficult. Yet others take fright at mathematics, or have reading difficulties. This is a society where the latter two are more of a problem than the others. These can all be real difficulties, but in other societies this would not necessarily be so. As the demands of society change, so do the learning disabilities. It may be that in the future a difficulty with computer studies might generate the sort of alarm that dyslexia does at the moment.

Learning and Performance

Finally, how do we measure learning? Only in a very rough and ready way by what the learner can actually show us in his performance. Learning itself is invisible.

There is a diagram generally known as the 'Learning Curve' (figure 4); it shows how performance tends to improve in leaps, rather than smoothly. However, despite its title, it does not show learning at all, it measures performance. Performance is to do with measurable results, and is not the same as learning. Learning is the process by which we gain insights and the ability to use them, and consequently widen our degree of choice.

The shape of the 'performance curve' is worth remembering when students do not seem to make any evident progress for some time. They will be on a plateau and will improve, if they wish to, given time, but it is impossible to predict when. Students can remember this too, so that they do not become discouraged if they are working hard but do not seem to be getting any better.

Performance

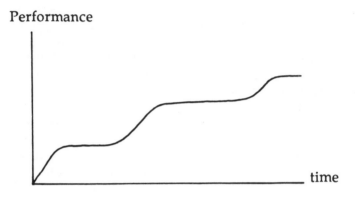

time

Figure 4

Most learning takes place on a deep, unconscious level.
Ideas and actions need time to sink in and really become
part of the range of skills we feel we can count on. The
Russians have a saying that we learn to ski in the
summer and swim in the winter. In other words skills
need time to develop and may develop faster if left
completely alone for a time. Our mind has a chance to
work over what has been learned and relate it to what we
already know. "Sleeping on a problem" is a similar idea
over a shorter time span. I find my students have often
made dramatic progress after a holiday, especially the
long summer one. Often they have done little playing.

It is quite possible to learn something and decide not
to do anything about it. In other words, the last and most
important step is the choice of how to act, or indeed
whether to act at all. The fact that we remember and understand something does not compel us to perform it.

Despite what the graph shows, learning is taking place
all the time, and is probably at its greatest on the plateaus.
Improved performance comes later. It is impossible to
separate learning from life itself.

Chapter Four

Initial Learning

A teacher's ability to see the student's point of view, or put himself in the student's place, will avoid many misunderstandings. By remembering what it was like not to have all the knowledge and experience he has now, the teacher will be in a better position to appreciate the meaning of the student's questions. It is difficult for us to remember parts of an action and to explain something with which we are very familiar. We are liable to forget how music appears to someone without this experience.

I can remember how very difficult it was for me to stretch across to get a G major chord when I first began playing the guitar. I remember too how it seemed impossible simultaneously to get a G sharp on string six at the same time as a G sharp on string three. I also have not-so-fond memories of the infamous left hand stretch in the Bach D minor Prelude BWV 999. I could not understand the principle of dotted notes for a long time and misread notes with leger lines. These are clear memories. Being aware of these feelings, I am more likely to understand if my students have similar difficulties, and help them with my personal memories and experience.

Other confusions will be obvious from the start. Making the lines of the stave correspond with the strings of the guitar is a favourite mistake, the up and down of the strings another. Although the first string is highest in pitch, it is the one nearest the floor when one holds the guitar correctly. It is normally called the top string. When we move from position one to position five, are we moving up or down the fingerboard? I have to explain that up and down is used in relation to pitch and moving up the guitar will involve going to higher frets nearer the soundhole.

Younger students are often confused into thinking that the direction of a note stem is significant in some way. Somehow notes look different if the stems go up rather than down. They have been taught that this sort of difference is very important in the alphabet, or 'pappy' would be the same as 'daddy'

Words like rhythm, beat, accent and stress are used in all sorts of confusing and contradictory ways. This is one area where teachers and books are inconsistent, and we need to clarify these terms to students in advance.

Strategies

Starting to read music and becoming in tune with a musical instrument means slowly building many complex skills. The task can seem overwhelming at the start. Beginners need some way of making sense of the music and building a dependable technique. They need a strategy, a process, a sequence of actions that uses their internal as well as their external senses to play the instrument and to remember the musical system. They will spend a great deal of time practising these skills and they need to use this time as efficiently as possible.

Teachers must teach a learning strategy; a sequence of senses used externally or internally. Some people typically talk to themselves a great deal before coming to a decision, others will go by their intuitive 'feel' for the situation. Others might construct pictures of the desired result, talk to themselves about ways to achieve it and feel satisfied when they have found a solution. This sequence would be visual , auditory, kinaesthetic. This is a simple example of a strategy.

Here is an example of the strategy used by good spellers. A word needs to be visualised to be spelt correctly. English is not a phonetic language. "Foenetick" spellings are likely to be wrong. Sounding the word out internally does not work well: "ghoti" could be a phonetic spelling of 'fish'- gh as in 'cough', o as in 'women' and ti as in 'condition'.

Most good spellers use the same strategy. They picture the word and check if it 'feels' right. The process must involve visualization, followed by a kinaesthetic check. Teaching spelling is easy. What is required is to make sure that words are remembered visually. Then spelling a word involves visually constructing different spellings until one matches the remembered image. This will 'feel' correct. You can just teach the process, there is no need for long tedious spelling tests. The right strategy enables anyone to become a good speller.

Another example is reading. Most people learn to read auditorily by reading aloud, before reading silently. Internalised reading aloud is slow. To read quickly, words have to be understood by sight alone, that is what 'speedreading' is all about.

So it is the form of the strategy, or process, which determines the degree of success. NLP is concerned with discovering successful and effective strategies, which can be taught to anyone, to give a better way of approaching a task. This is true learning. Practice does not make perfect. Experience is not the same as competence. Repeating an action many times will not necessarily improve it past a certain point, if the strategy is not an effective one. Adults who have spelt words auditorily for years may be worse spellers than children who have been doing it for a fraction of that time using a visual strategy. Teaching strategies for doing tasks is a more elegant and effective way than presenting content and hoping the student has a good strategy to make sense of it.

If I want to find out how to perform a complex skill such as playing a musical instrument, I would find someone who already does it well. I would closely observe him, see what he does on the process level, and ask him specific questions about how he does it. Then I would go and do the same, applying the process to the particular music that I want to play. This is modelling a skill, and is the obvious course of action when dealing with visible external techniques. The teacher needs to be just such a model. If you wish to learn something efficiently, take someone who learns quickly and easily as your model. Copy his strategy. NLP provides some powerful ways to do this. A teacher can pass on the external model (technique), and the internal model (the learning process). Both are essential.

Learning to Read Music

What is the best strategy for learning to read music?
The starting point is a stave containing symbols which
indicate the pitch and duration of notes.

Each note also has a letter name from A to G. This is
the shorthand way to indicate pitch, and it needs to be
known. The exact letter name of the note depends firstly on
the clef at the beginning of the music, and secondly, on the
position of the note on the stave.

When a beginner is reading easy guitar music, he is
recognising familiar visual patterns (notes on the stave),
and linking them with a finger placement on the guitar.
The note must be recognised by sight alone. Musicians
know what a note is because they have seen it before.

Reading music is like reading words. Both involve
powers of recognition. Notes and words are seen externally and recognised by matching them to a remembered internal image. The letter name of a note is an integral part of
this process of recognition and with practice and time the
knowledge will become second nature. The letter name
must not enter consciousness at all if music reading is to be
fluent. In the same way we are not aware of the individual
letters when we read words. We know them of course, but
they are small chunks and have been incorporated into
much larger ones. For a strategy to become quick and easy,
most of the steps must be made unconscious, but they
must be consciously and carefully learned at first.

If reading music is like reading words and involves
recognition, then writing music is like spelling and
involves recall. It is not necessary to be a good speller to
read well, and many younger students can read music, but
cannot accurately write down from memory what they
have just seen and played correctly. They can go from
visual to kinaesthetic, (note to finger placement), but not

necessarily in the opposite direction.

Being able to recall notes is considerably easier than spelling. The musical system follows formal, regular patterns which can be worked out in advance from first principles in a way that spelling never can.

I think that music must be learned in small enough chunks to be recalled and written down, as well as recognised. This writing down and recall is an essential part of learning. It can be done by asking students to take a 'mental photograph' of a small number of notes with which they are already familiar, then to write them down from the eidetic image. Directing their eyes up and left will often help if they are not doing this already. Accessing cues will show if they are visualising. Their check will either be kinaesthetic (feeling that it is right) or auditory (usually internal dialogue). This process is essentially the same as teaching spelling. It will also strengthen their powers of visualization.

Music is a logical system and the parts will rapidly fall into place as the chunking becomes more complex. Any student who has not used an internal visual process will literally have a "fuzzy" understanding. This stage must precede finger placement, (although it can be taught simultaneously with it), because finger placement is directly dependent on the letter name.

Anything that hinders this process of learning to read music is not helpful. This is why I do not think it is a good idea for children to write the letter names of the notes underneath them. Many children do this in the initial stages of learning. These letters are useful as a reminder, but if they are necessary for a performance, then the student is no longer reading music, but letters. He may be lost without these letters, for he is relying on a particular extra visual stimulus which is not an organic part of the music. Such a system will inevitably break down as the music becomes more complicated. It is a doubling and splitting up of the information contained in the note symbol which must provide an internal link with its letter name, not have an external, written one.

For the same reasons I do not think a system of colour-

coded notes is helpful in the long run. Colour is a variable
that is not needed and in fact makes the task more complex,
for it   adds   another step in the process of recognition.
Instead of progressing by note > letter name > position on
guitar, the sequence becomes note > colour > letter name >
position on guitar. Or even worse, colour > letter name >
position on guitar. Worst of all is colour > position on
guitar. In this latter case reading pitch will be fuzzy as the
student will not need to see exactly where the note is on the
stave to know its letter name and position, the colour is
enough. The whole idea breaks down in a polychromatic
blur as the music grows in complexity. I have seen students
with guitars festooned with coloured stickers and it does not
seem to help them in the slightest.

Children normally start by associating the position of the
note on the stave directly with a particular string and fret
on the guitar. This is coding the note kinaesthetically and is
a   good initial strategy, providing the letter name is
known too. At this early stage it is not necessary to know
the principle of the chromatic scale or very much abstract
music theory to explain why a note is played on a particular
fret. This comes later, and with it the ability to work out any
note on the guitar fingerboard. Adults   will   quickly,
sometimes immediately, come to terms with these ideas,
but children have a more empirical approach. Adults tend
to understand the particular by applying the general idea;
while children learn by working more from the particular
towards the abstract principles.

I would like to summarise a good strategy for learning
to read music. As a model of what good musicians do, it
can be taught step by step to instrumental students. This
model will start with the smallest possible chunk; reading a
single note.

Firstly the note is seen using the visual sense externally.
It is understood by comparing it with an internal
remembered visual image to determine its letter name.
This internal visual memory forms the basis of recognising,
deciphering, recalling and composing new pieces.

The next step is actually stopping the guitar string with
a left hand finger, (unless it is an open string), and striking

it with a right hand finger. This uses the kinaesthetic sense externally. The finger movements are coded into muscle memory by repeated playings. These form the basis of the internal kinaesthetic check that the finger is in the right place. It is the guide to fast accurate finger movements.

Thirdly, we use the auditory sense externally (we hear the note) and check that it is correct by comparing it with an internal auditory memory of what we expect to hear from our musical experience and sense of relative pitch. We already have a general internal auditory representation of a diatonic major and minor scale from growing up in a western European culture where music is largely based on these scales.

This internal auditory sense takes time to build, unless a student already has perfect pitch. Students will blithely play notes out of key that set a musician's teeth on edge, because they lack his auditory discrimination.

Here is a diagram of the complete strategy :

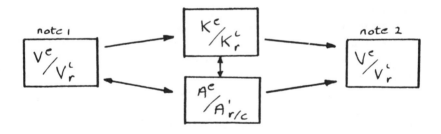

Figure 5

Ve Visual external (seeing the note)
V^i_r Visual internal remembered (knowledge of the note and letter name)
K^e Kinaesthetic external (finger movements)
K^i_r Kinaesthetic internal remembered (muscle memory)
A^e Auditory external (hearing the note)
$A^i_{r/c}$ Auditory internal constructed or remembered (expectation of the sound)

When A^e does not match with $A^i{}_{r/c}$ there will be a check back to the finger placement (K^e) and the note (V^e).

This is the final strategy and it takes time to form. It is simplified, it takes no account of interpretation, tone and feeling. These all come at a higher level and will change the A^i which in turn will modify the K^e step. Vibrato is a good example. Nor does the diagram take timing into account. This would involve an overall view of at least two of these diagrams. Timing is at a higher level of organization than pitch. It determines the temporal relationship between at least two notes, and would need to incorporate a check between two consecutive versions of Figure 1. The great pianist Artur Schnabel is reported to have said, "A musician sees with his ears and hears with his eyes." Perhaps this is the most elegant summing up of the strategy.

The more steps that are unconscious, the faster and more fluent the process. The sequence is almost simultaneous in an accomplished player. It is so habitual that he could hardly prevent himself from recognising, playing and expecting the right note. As a player becomes more competent, all these steps are organised into more complex chunks. For example the visual input could be a chord or a scale fragment, and not just a single note.

Learning to read music involves repeatedly using the three senses outwardly to make reliable internal representations which are used to check further musical work. The teacher's role is to make sure that these are well formed at every stage. He must make sure the student knows the name of the note from an internal visual picture. He must make sure the correct finger response is coded in muscle memory and that good technical habits are acquired. He must make sure that the internal auditory sense is developed so that the sound can be checked. While the student is learning, the teacher will supply these three checks externally. He will point out mistakes in reading music. He will see that the student's fingers move freely and easily round the fingerboard, and he will say if the sound is wrong. He will also refine the sound by asking for such things as good tone, articulation and dynamics.

Some students find it extremely difficult to play a piece unless they have heard it before. They are "playing by ear" to a great extent; their music reading is uncertain. They have a strategy like this:

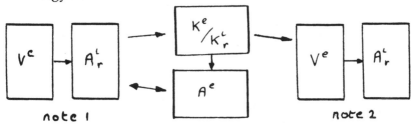

Figure 6

One player I knew went through an internal cycle to find any note. He remembered what two or three notes looked like on the stave and where to play them on the guitar. He had learned a scale that connected the notes he knew with those he did not. When he came to a note he did not know, he would start with a note he knew and mentally read up the stave a line and a space at a time while mentally playing until he had reached the note he wanted. He would then play the string and finger he had reached. This is like being able to identify a number by counting up to it from one, instead of knowing what it is from its appearance. He used this very long-winded way of playing because he had been overloaded with notes at an early stage of learning.

The fact that he was able to do this process confirms my belief that people become very adept at the strategies they use. Minds work incredibly fast. What determines success is whether the strategy being followed is an elegant, effective one.

Any acquired skill can be analysed in these terms and to a greater degree than I have done here. Teachers can guide students through this initial learning process and not leave them to their own devices. If a student is having difficulty learning to read music, he is probably using an inefficient strategy. If you can discover what this is, then you can change it.

Looking at the Fingerboard

We are conditioned to think that we must see something to be sure of it; but to play the guitar freely, the hands have to judge distance by touch alone. The eyes have their 'hands full' reading the music. Many beginners will look away from the music to check their hands and so lose their place. Even music known by heart needs to be playable by touch. Listening gives the feedback for any adjustments.

Many students use an external visual check: they look at the fingerboard to see if they have put their left hand fingers in the right place. To do this, they have to take their eyes off the music and risk losing their place. Some students visually check the right hand fingers too - so look in three different places before playing a note; a very complicated and tiring business!

They have a strategy like this:

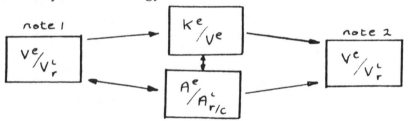

Figure 7

Finding your way round the fingerboard by touch is a better choice than having to look because you will not lose your place in the music. A highly visual person might find this difficult at first. Some of my students use a internal visual check: when asked to play scales without looking, they stare upwards and form an internal picture of the fingerboard, then mentally watch their fingers moving on it to check they are in the right place. I found this out by asking them what they were doing when I saw them looking up. I was able completely to disrupt the playing of one advanced student by asking him to look downwards and not upwards while he played a simple scale. This cannot be a good strategy if playing can be so easily disturbed!

A good way for a student to cross from visual to

kinaesthetic is to pay attention first to his feeling sense while actually looking at his left hand on the fingerboard. He will not be able to play without looking if he has not developed some discrimination in his sense of spatial awareness and he cannot do this without help initially. His way forward is to continue to look at the fingerboard, but to be aware of his fingers as he does so; then he can aim to reproduce the feeling of spreading his fingers without the visual check. Instead, he must make a kinaesthetic map. He can move from what he sees to what he feels. It is best for a player to look down and to the right when he is working on muscle memory.

I think looking at the left hand lies at the root of many postural problems that plague guitarists. It leads to the front of the body shortening and twisting to the left. The guitar will tilt backwards, so that its front angles upwards. The whole balance of the body is disturbed.

One student bent her left thumb over the top of the guitar in a violin grip, and so could not reach the. bass notes easily. Her left hand was pulled back because the guitar was tilted towards her. She told me she tilted it in order to see the fingerboard. When I asked her to straighten the guitar so it was at right angles to the floor, her left hand was automatically corrected. Her left hand position was correct. It was just the guitar angle that was wrong. If I had tried to correct the left hand in isolation, it would have put her arm into a very awkward position.

This preoccupation with looking at the fingerboard is unnecessary. In our everyday life we judge perspective from all sorts of angles and adjust our movements accordingly. It is quite possible to keep an eye on the left hand while keeping the body erect and balanced. This is done with peripheral vision; using the 'corner of the eye'. Peripheral vision is actually better at judging movement than looking at things more directly. The light-sensitive cells towards the edges of the retina are better at detecting movement than those in the middle.

I asked my student to look straight ahead and held up my hand in front of her, then moved it slowly round until it was at right angles to her and asked her to tell me when she could not see it any more. She said it was visible right up to the last moment. I knew it would be, and I wanted to demonstrate this. The angle of eye to left hand on the guitar is always less than ninety degrees, so there is no real problem. Perhaps it is just anxiety about making mistakes that leads to this visual overkill. Peripheral vision is trustworthy and quite enough to cope with any difficult left hand jumps.

An extended example of one student may help to explain these strategies. Helen had been learning the guitar with me for about two years at secondary school. She also played the double-bass in the school jazz band. She had passed grade five theory of music independently a year before. We were studying quite complex music together, but she was increasingly making elementary mistakes. Her timing was good, but she was playing wrong notes more and more frequently and often seemed to be puzzled when I corrected her. She was misreading basic notes and I was intrigued. I had to find out what she was doing at a process level, or lessons would become one long round of corrections.

Over the next few lessons, I found out what Helen was doing. She did not have any precise idea of the letter names of many of the notes which she was playing. She did know the letter names of a few notes on the stave (specifically c and c') and used them laboriously to work out others if necessary. She was not clear about the notes of the guitar open strings. Once upon a time she knew them, but they had slipped from her mind through disuse.

She had built up a vocabulary of notes on the guitar by translating a particular musical symbol directly to a specific left hand finger position. So instead of going through the full sequence: note on the stave equals 'd' (for example), which can be played on the second string, third fret, she left out the intermed ate step and the symbol on the stave was translated straight to the finger position. By leaving out this middle stage (the letter name of the note) she was not able to work out that the same note could also be played on the third string seventh fret, and also on the fourth string twelfth fret. To be able to do this, she would have to know the note is 'd', and also to know the notes of the third and fourth open strings. Otherwise, although the three different positions for 'd' can be learned by rote as finger movements, they will seem quite arbitrary.

Many students decide that they can do without letter names at first, but later, although there may be gaps in their knowledge, they usually have a good idea of the musical system independent of the guitar. It is like making the transition from being able to count on your fingers to having an appreciation of number as a concept.

Although Helen had not played the recorder for two years, her immediate reaction to seeing a note on the treble clef was not a letter name, or even a guitar fingering, but a memory of the finger movement that would play the note on the treble recorder. She had learnt the treble recorder when she was much younger and it had obviously made a lasting impression on her.

She had managed to go a considerable way before I called her bluff. It made me wonder how learning strategies are hidden because they work up to a point. The teacher may assume everybody is taking the same steps he followed. The student may assume that the way he is learning is correct, because it comes easily and awkward questions can be avoided, or are never asked. If the student is not doing well, then it may be assumed that he is either stupid, or not working hard enough at what the teacher thinks he is doing.

Helen was a fluent reader of the bass clef on the double-bass. She would sometimes read a note in the treble clef as if it were in the bass clef. Furthermore, she would often then go on and play a double-bass left hand fingering on the guitar! She did this consistently with the note:

This is a 'd' on the treble clef, and located, as I have said, on the second string, third fret. On the bass clef the same note is 'f'. It is located on the double bass in precisely the same position; string two, fret three! So Helen would end up playing the correct note on the guitar even though the process she went through was mistaken at every turn. Different clef, different letter name, different instrument! I think this a wonderful example of how the end result can be totally misleading about the process used to achieve it.

So there were important gaps in Helen's playing strategy. She told me that her first guitar tutor was full of finger numbers, so she used them right from the start.

Helen could play well in the first position in standard guitar keys of up to four sharps. She had a very good sense of relative pitch, which she used to check her playing. In fact, I doubt if she would have got as far as she did without it.

She was very good at identifying the interval between two notes by matching it against her clear internal auditory memory. She did this to   make   sure that what   she actually heard herself play corresponded with what she ex-pected to hear. She was getting into difficulties now, be-cause the music was becoming more complicated. Firstly, this taxed her kinaesthetic memory, and secondly the musical intervals involved were more difficult to hear internally. They were less likely to be diatonic, (found between two notes in the scale of the key of the piece), and more likely to be chromatic, (not limited to those found in the scale of the key of the piece). Sometimes chords were involved too, so there were more notes to play simultaneously and the aural checking was more complicated.

The musical note patterns were no longer as regular as they had been. A good deal of the guitar's easy early repertoire which she had played was from nineteenth century composers and was fairly predictable, both melodically and harmonically.

Helen's strategy was the opposite of that used by those students, who write letters underneath the notes and play from these. This method is easily visible, it is there in black and white on the paper, but Helen's kinaesthetic strategy was invisible.

I asked her which school subjects she enjoyed doing and which she found tiresome and difficult. She told me her mathematics was weak because she could not remember multiplication tables. She found them impossible to memorise by repetitive chanting, which was how she was taught them. She also told me that she had trouble learning the alphabet at primary school, again by chanting. She had devised ways herself to link letters visually so that she could easily recall them.

I can vividly remember chanting both the alphabet and multiplication tables at primary school. Luckily, I have a good sequential auditory memory and a strong internal auditory sense, so this worked for me. Many students need a visualising strategy successfully to learn both multiplication tables and the alphabet. Thinking back and noticing the adverb I used at the beginning of the paragraph (vividly), I do link the learning of both with a clear visual image of the places where I learnt them.

Helen had a good deal of artistic talent, her painting and design work was very elaborate, imaginative, and technically good. She was also good at English composition and History, where there was scope for her imagination and little constraint from answers which were right or wrong. She was good at improvisation on the double bass, where she used her excellent musical ear to fashion what she wanted to hear.

Helen had passed grade five theory of music by using, in her own words, "tricks and mnemonics". I think she meant she did not understand the material, but could remember it with these devices.

I felt she could use her talents to change her strategy for learning music and playing the guitar. I already knew that Helen's most highly valued representational system was kinaesthetic and what I had found certainly confirmed this. As she was good at art, it seemed to be a good idea to use her powers of visualization.

I suggested that she learn her multiplication tables by sight and the next week she showed me the art work she had done for this. The method worked well. We devised mnemomics for her to remember the notes of the guitar open strings and the notes on the stave. I left it to her to devise pictures that could be as elaborate and colourful as she wished to represent the notes on the stave and anything else she had difficulty remembering. If she forgot something, I asked her to see her drawing in her mind's eye again and make sure it included included the clef. In the lesson, I could check that she did so from her eye movements.

This visual approach helped her to decipher the notes on the stave and remember the guitar open strings. It was almost like starting again. Although this seemed tedious, I was sure, and more importantly, so was Helen, that when she could bring this knowledge and understanding to her already fluent left hand memory and aural appreciation, her playing would be immeasurably strengthened. I stressed again what I say to all my students: do not play a note if you do not know its letter name. Find this out first. Work it out or look it up.

Helen quickly replaced her previous strategy with one that involved the understanding and knowledge of the letter name of every note she played. She now knew the open strings, and with the principle of the chromatic scale, her knowledge was much more soundly based.

I gave her both diatonic and chromatic pieces that could be played not only in first position, but also in higher ones. She could no longer rely on her sense of relative pitch in chromatic tunes to check if she had played the right note. Playing the tunes in the different positions meant that her kinaesthetic memory of the finger movements in the first position could not help her. When playing in the higher unfamiliar positions, she still sometimes misread the notes, thinking they were on the bass clef, but now she was immediately aware when this happened.

I felt privileged that Helen had given me so much insight into how she learned. I found it incredibly interesting and it taught me a number of things. Open-mindedness is so important. There are no right answers that work for everyone and what is actually happening often bears no relation to what you think is happening. Teaching by result misses the most important and interesting part of the whole educational process. I certainly had been guilty of this, otherwise I would have seen what was happening earlier. Only the student knows the whole story. I will not take so much for granted in future.

The teacher can increase the student's area of choice. Perhaps this is all a teacher can ever do. The way forward is to balance and develop all the senses together. This gives the student more choice, and allows him to progress if he wishes to do so.

Students are bound to make mistakes and be unsure about notes. Some, like Helen, need to develop their visual memory. Others need kinaesthetic reinforcement of which finger to use. Adopting this latter approach with Helen would simply have strengthened her one-sided strategy. She already knew too well which fingers to use; what she was not clear about was why she was using them.

In fact, Helen seems to be someone who uses her right brain capabilities more than most people. She is strong on visualization, mnemonics, and musical memory. A sense of relative pitch is an appreciation of relationships between notes, not of the notes themselves, and therefore I think it is linked to the right brain rather than the left. Helen needed to bring in visualization and to balance her overall approach. She needed then to make more use of the analytical powers of the left brain, and to integrate the three main representational systems so they all worked equally together.

Aural Memory

Aural training is building up the auditory memory or "inner ear" for pitch and rhythm. Aural tests are only methods for finding out the accuracy of auditory memory and whether the student can reproduce what he has heard. They involve recall much more than recognition. With the use of representational systems and accessing cues I can often 'see' what a student is actually doing when he is using his "inner ear".

To give an example. I was teaching a secondary school student last year to play the melody of the Catalan Folk song 'El Noy de la Mare', and he was having great difficulty with

the recurring dotted crotchet rhythm in this beautiful
Spanish piece. I asked him simply to tap the rhythm on the
guitar. Trying to find the notes as well was confusing him
even further. He had trouble working out the rhythm for
himself, so I tapped it out and asked him to copy me, but he
found even this difficult. I was convinced there was
nothing wrong with his auditory memory, and that he
would succeed if I could change the way he approached the
problem, so I decided to experiment.

Across the room to his left there was a clock on the wall. I
asked him to look at it out of the corner of his eye without
turning his head. I tapped out the rhythm again and asked
him to repeat it to me. He did so immediately. I tapped
some different, more complex rhythms. He repeated them
without hesitation. He was surprised, and so was I! He told
me weeks later that he remembers rhythms easily if he
looks across to his left.

This seems like magic. There appears to be no link at all
between cause and effect; but I had noticed that his eyes
went strongly across to his right as he tried to reproduce the
rhythm which I had tapped out for him. In order to reproduce it correctly he had to remember it, in other words to be
able to represent it accurately to himself from auditory
memory. Gary's eye movements followed the usual
pattern: left to remember and right to construct. His eye
movements suggested that instead of trying to remember
the rhythm, he might be trying to construct it in some way.

He had to turn his eyes across to his left in order to look
at the clock. I think this had at least three very valuable
results. Firstly, it broke up the current unsuccessful strategy,
and forced him to do something else. Secondly, his eye
movements may have been linked with his powers of
auditory memory rather than those of auditory
construction. Turning his eyes to the left stimulated the
right side of the retina, which is linked to the right side of
the brain, and his powers of rhythmic memory. Thirdly, by
making such a seemingly ridiculous demand I got him to
be curious instead of anxious, and broke the cycle of
trying harder and failing.

This method worked for Gary. I used the same method

with another student a few weeks later, with the same result. This is not a bizarre panacea for improving rhythmic memory. Eye movements are only the outward clues to an inward process. What matters is to notice what is happening, and to experiment in order to change the student's way of approaching a problem. Directing a person's eyes in the appropriate direction will often facilitate the use of a particular internal sense.

Aural Tests

Students will have to respond to aural tests in music examinations, but the development of the "inner ear" is important in its own right. When I work with students on – rhythmic memory, I play or tap a rhythm and ask them to play it back mentally, but not to tap it back immediately.

This internal recreation of the rhythm must come from the internal auditory sense. I can   check   that this is happening from the eye accessing cues (provided I know the student's characteristic eye responses in the first place), and also from breathing changes.

It may be necessary initially to use the student's strongest sense to lead into auditory memory. So if the student is a strong visualiser, it may be helpful for him to make a picture of me playing the music on the piano and proceed from that to hearing the sound internally. I might ask him to imagine himself tapping the rhythm. This will bring in the visual and kinaesthetic sense. This sort of refinement depends on the individual students.

I then tap or play the rhythm again and ask him to check what he heard mentally with what he hears now. Only then does he tap it back to me. This approach works equally well with pitch.

Aural tests assume the student is a musical 'black box'. The test goes in one side, there is some mysterious activi-ty in the middle, and out pops the response. Success in aural tests is not just due to an inborn "musical ear". With NLP techniques aural memory is no longer invisible.

It is also important for students to be able to tell the difference between the sound of a major and minor   chord, the two basic types of chord from which others are built. This is sometimes used in examinations as an aural recognition test.

I have noticed that if I ask a student, without any prompting, how he would describe the sound of a major chord, he will often answer in visual language. It is often described as "bright". When I ask how he perceives a minor chord, a common answer is that it is "sadder" and this is a kinaesthetic word. No wonder then, that the student will find it difficult to tell the difference between major and minor chords, because he is not comparing them in the same frame of reference. It is of great benefit to know the preferred representational system of each student. Major and minor chords can be described in visual terms, eg. "bright" and "dark", or kinaesthetic terms, eg. "happy" and "sad". Once these are reliably established, they can be used as a bridge leading to a purely auditory representation, where chords are compared with an auditory memory. This can be checked by observing accessing cues.

A great deal of music educational method is merely a reflection of the proposer's preferred representational system. Some fascinating research is being done, for this is still new territory for musicians. I hope I have given some stimulating ideas for further work.

Chapter Five

Practice

Practice. This word normally crops up several times a page in any discussion on instrumental playing. My dictionary defines practice as ".....perform habitually, carry out an action, exercise oneself in or on an instrument, exercise or pursue a profession......." My students defined the word differently when I asked what it meant to them. What they understand by this key word is very important. There will be a communication breakdown if a teacher takes a word to mean one thing and students understand it to mean another. I think this happens regularly and under-lies many students' accusations of unfairness about their teachers and teachers' accusations of stupidity about their students.

I will sum up their collective definition of practice. It was repetitive, it isolated and concentrated on the difficult sections. It aimed at improvement and was not much fun. It was something you had to do in order to play well. It was almost a chore that had to be done to make progress towards a promised land where they would be able to "play the guitar". Practice was contrasted with simply playing through the piece without stopping, which was something you could do only after you had practised it. Not all students thought this way, but I do not believe my sample of student attitudes was wildly eccentric. Even so, if I am going to tell them to practise, it is a good idea to find out what it means to them, and so what they are going to do.

The way we use the words 'practice' and 'playing', or at least the way they are often understood, encourages an arbitrary distinction between playing at different times, and in different ways. The actual words do not matter; it is the state of mind that they induce that is important. Practise for what? Surely either you play the guitar or you do not. Playing is best done and enjoyed most by attending to what you do, listening to the result, and taking pleasure in the whole process. It does not matter if the music you are playing is a small phrase, or a whole sonata. As time passes certain passages become more fluent, phrasing is shaped, interpretation moulded, and the whole piece gains life and momentum in a continual creative process. Each time the music is played, you play it the best you can at that particular moment, with full attention. This is the way to enjoy and improve.

Practice is also understood to mean hard work, but work is 'hard' depending on a person's state of mind. What is hard to one person is an enjoyable challenge to another. It is true that certain phrases in any piece will need to be worked on more than others, because they are technically or musically more difficult, otherwise a piece will be very uneven because it has always been played from the beginning with no discrimination about which parts need more work than others.

Practice can become synonymous with what is done hunched over a music stand at home, worthwhile only because it leads to an actual performance on stage, or in front of the teacher. No wonder students get so nervous. All that work is suddenly on trial.

The attitude that the word 'practice' seems to generate, at least in my experience of music students, has turned its meaning upside down. To practise medicine does not mean to try it out with a view to improvement, otherwise there would be a lot of malpractice suits (taken up by practising lawyers).

Such is the power of words. Practice can acquire many negative connotations, sometimes the very mention of the word is enough to make a student mentally wince. It can easily take on the character of a compulsory, and unpleasant activity. Many students did not seem to believe that practice was actually making music. Their state of mind when they 'practised' was different to when they 'played'. 'Practice' was not always pleasant, while 'playing' usually was. Words have great power to evoke different states of mind. I do not wish to put students in a rather heavy, uncomfortable state of mind by telling them to practise. Simply by using a different word, I can put them in a more positive frame of mind about the work I will invite them to do at home. Once again, the meaning of the communication is the response it evokes.

"Practice makes perfect" is a saying I dislike particularly. Practice makes perfunctory might be more accurate. Practice is a nominalization. What and how is a student practising? The saying also has the judge missing (who is deciding the perfection?) and the verb is unspecified (makes what or who perfect?). There is also an implied cause and effect (makes), and the subject has been deleted (who is practising?) I would be hard pressed to find another phrase that has so many Meta Model violations. It is a remarkably vague saying! I know that such folk wisdom is not meant to be analysed so minutely. I am taking it as a starting point to investigate the crucial elements of practice.

All these Meta Model questions do not have equal importance. The cause-effect link needs qualifying. Simple repetition will not improve a piece if what you repeat is mistaken or the technique you use is faulty. Repeating nonsense will achieve fluent, thoughtless nonsense. It is not worth repeating something you do not think is worthwhile, and the time will be wasted anyway if you are tired and unable to concentrate.

Practice for me means the process of building reliable internal representations about music and the instrument from the repeated outward use of the senses, by the process described in the last chapter. Auditory and visual memories are built up and strengthened and muscle memory is reinforced. To do this, the senses must be directed outwards, paying exact attention to the sounds, the sight of the notes and the muscular feelings and movements of the fingers of both hands. All practice is playing really, and all playing practice. Nor can these technical matters be isolated from such things as creativity, emotions and beauty of sound which gives music such great power to move.

How to practise is the most important missing information. We need to pay attention to each and every repetition on the instrument. This is difficult to remember if we play a passage many times. We may say to our students or ourselves, "Let's do it once again." I suggest a change of emphasis in this phrase to "Let's do it *once* again." In other words treat each time as the first time and keep paying attention.   Play it as well as you possibly can. This way of playing by-passes the idea of mindless, boring repetition that many players believe is necessary to improve a piece.

Musicians are people who have developed their ability to listen. It is difficult to listen carefully, but not in the sense that it needs a lot of trying and effort, in fact these make it impossible. Awareness, particularly careful listening will improve any performance. When we listen to a sound we somehow give it life. Many times I have only to ask a student to listen to her playing for the tone to improve. This pays her the compliment of allowing her to decide and alter her sound if it is not good. I find this a better method than simply telling her to improve the tone, for then she is liable to guess what I mean and will probably forget immediately after the lesson.

Playing with little awareness will be less effective and expressive and   take much longer to realise the musical aims. Half an hour of playing with awareness is worth six hours of playing without. It is probably impossible to play six hours a day with awareness anyway, in which case the best to be hoped for is that this marathon does no harm. At worst overpractice   will   simply   undo the good already achieved.

Time like money, is used as a shorthand measure of worth, but time spent on a project or article is not a reliable measure of its value. Two hours playing a day is not twice as good as one hour. Time and money can be exactly quantified, attention cannot. There is an apocryphal story about a famous guitarist who was only able to play for half an hour a day while on National Service. None the less, when discharged two years later, he had lost none of his playing skill He knew how to make the best use of his very limited playing time. The way forward does not lie in doing some foolproof set of exercises; improvement guaranteed, or money refunded, superficially attractive as this might be. Nor does it lie in practising six hours a day. These two approaches are reflections of each other, and equally unrealistic. Both ignore the quality of the player's attention.

Habits

Repeating actions and paying attention to the feedback will eventually form habits. The process of acquiring a skill has three stages, each blending into the next.

Firstly, you discover the skill, start to practise it and find you are not very proficient. This is the demoralising stage of conscious incompetence, but it is when the most learning and change is taking place. This brings you eventually to the stage of conscious competence. Here you are proficient at the skill, but it is liable to be slow and you have to keep thinking about it as you do it.

Lastly, and the goal of your endeavour, is the stage of unconscious competence where the actions are automatic, they have become habitual and your attention is free to engage in something else.

This is a simplified scheme, different skill components are liable to be at different stages, but the first two stages: the conscious ones, are the only places where changes and learning can take place. A habit is a product of the third stage and must be taken back to the previous one for re-examination if it is to be changed.

Habits have both a physical and a mental dimension, the two cannot be separated. All physical actions have a mental counterpart. The visible, demonstrable results of instrumental technique are physical, but to form them in the first place, or alter them once formed, involves a mental change.

Habits are the unreflecting use of past experience in the present and are useful if the past experience has been carefully built up with discrimination, and is relevant to the present. This applies to physical guitar technique, but not to a live teaching situation where the teacher must respond to the needs of the present moment.

Habits deserve a good deal of respect. They are great energy savers and release attention for other things: phrasing, articulation and interpretation for example. Performers want to have conscious control over these, so that they may vary them from performance to performance. On the other hand, they want their technical control to remain dependably the same. They do not even want to be aware of it.

A faulty technical habit often hinders expressive playing. It will become set if we think "Just once more like this won't hurt, next time I will do it right". This does not mean that a habit will become set in a few trials, but it will solidify eventually if we take this attitude for long enough. Make sure that the best way becomes easiest to do. Aiming for this will take you through the conscious incompetence stage without mishap.

It does take a long time to form habits. The way that students hold the guitar and use their hands at the first lesson, is an expression of the total way they use their body. It is already based on habit. I have noticed instrumental teachers often seem to have a special view of habits, for they act as if good habits take years of patient hard work to build up, but bad habits take seconds to acquire, and must be instantly corrected or all is lost. They are in far too much of a hurry to correct a student's mistakes. If a student does have difficulty co-ordinating in an effective way, this is a reflection of his total body use, which did not appear overnight and is not going to change overnight either.

We learn by a sequence of successive approximations. Step by step we get as close as we can to what we want, all the time gaining more control of the use of the muscles involved. It is not a case of all right or all wrong. Childrens' muscles have to mature, and forcing them too early can do more harm than good. It is better not to be in a hurry to correct students' mistakes, but it takes courage and trust not to interfere.

In any activity, it is best to be as aware as possible, and alive to the messages our senses send us. We can only do this by being awake in the present moment. Habits can become another aspect of being aware and choosing what to do. In this case choosing to form or use a habit.

Chapter Six

The Alexander Technique

There is an approach to physical habits and use of the body that operates with the principles that I have outlined; widening a person's horizons and degree of choice, concentration on the process of change, experimentation and awareness. It is called the Alexander Technique. It is valued in theatrical, educational, and musical circles as a method of psychophysical re-education. It interested me originally by claiming to show how to use the body in a relaxed and effective way to overcome habitual patterns of bodily misuse that interfere with poise and free movement. I found my own experience certainly bore out these claims.

The Alexander Technique is named after its founder, Frederick Matthias Alexander, who was born in Australia in 1869. He studied Music and Drama at Melbourne and started his own amateur dramatic company. In his twenties, he established himself as a notable actor and recitalist, but he soon began to experience a good deal of difficulty with his voice; he suffered from persistent hoarseness and respiratory trouble. His voice would fail during important performances, and the remedies and diagnoses he obtained from the various doctors he consulted did not help. His career and livelihood were threatened if the trouble did not clear, so he was particularly well motivated to find the answer for himself.

He started to observe closely what he did with his body when reciting. He noticed that he stiffened his neck, which caused his head to be pulled backwards and down. This in turn depressed his larynx and led him to suck in air through his mouth rather than breathe naturally. He found this happened in ordinary conversation too, but to a much lesser degree. He keenly felt the importance and pressure of being a successful recitalist on professional occasions; this made him nervous and amplified his everyday habits of speech, thus causing his voice to fail.

Alexander found that he tended to lift his chest and narrow his back as well as stiffening his neck. This combination of actions meant that he did not stand his full height. He continued to experiment and found that his voice improved when he stood his full height and allowed his head to go forward and up from his body. This crucial head/neck/body relationship he called primary control.

By working from a specific problem, Alexander came to far-reaching conclusions about the use of his whole body; for all actions are connected to, and expressive of, the whole personality. Changing patterns of body use is like pulling one end of a tangled ball of wool; it will ultimately unravel the whole skein. A 'loose end' cannot be tidied up in isolation. To try to change a habit without taking this into account simply sets up counter-pressures elsewhere. I can see this when my attempts to relax a student's hand in a guitar lesson result in increased tension in his shoulders. We function as a whole, and are changed as a whole. Another metaphor would be to throw a stone into a pool, the ripples will radiate out to affect the whole expanse of water.

Alexander thought he had reached the answer. He attempted to recite while positively lengthening his neck, and preventing himself from shortening his stature. To his surprise, he found he could not. The habits of a lifetime were not so easily disposed of. He found he actually did the opposite of what he intended to do; at the critical moment he actually put his head back and shortened his neck despite his good intentions. He could see this clearly by working with mirrors. He wrote later of the delusion we suffer from, thinking we can 'will' or 'try' to do something that is contrary to our ingrained physical habits; that is, the basic way we use ourselves. We can will actions that are habitual easily enough; they almost happen by themselves, they have been put on 'automatic pilot', but working against habit means that we are dealing with unfamiliar physical sensations. We are not very good at evaluating unfamiliar physical sensations. They feel wrong, though in fact they are simply new. What we are used to feels right. So comfort backs up familiarity - a formidable combination!

Alexander found that the proprioceptive sense, or sense of our own bodies, can be unreliable when we are dealing with habits. We do not always do what we think we are doing. Habits need energy to form, and having been formed, feel familiar and right. Habits that are unnatural to our bodies take more energy to form, but feel just as right and familiar and are equally out of awareness. He used the marvellous phrase "Debauched Kinaesthesia" to describe this state of being deceived by familiar feelings.

When I first took Alexander lessons, my main concern was to find a comfortable and efficient way of holding the guitar for myself and for my students. Poor posture is reflected in tension in the hands and this hampers speed and co-ordination. It is also tiring. I hoped I might find an answer to the great problem of backache for guitarists, who spend a great deal of time sitting holding an awkwardly shaped piece of wood, trying to stop it slipping off their lap. This can lead to some strange bodily contortions and consequent backache.

This was admittedly a rather modest aim, for I did not appreciate at the time how all the actions we do are expressive of our total body use and habits cannot be changed in isolation. It soon became clear to me that some of the habitual ways I used my body were not very good and this was so whatever I did. Playing the guitar is only one rather specialised activity; I had to change my physical awareness at a much more fundamental level, and I stopped taking my guitar to my Alexander lesson.

Posture

Good posture is very important for all musicians. I know the postural problems of guitarists best so I will consider them in detail. The usual way for a right-handed classical guitarist to sit involves resting the left leg on an adjustable footstool. The guitar is then balanced with its waist resting on the left thigh, while the right leg prevents it from slipping down to the right.

Figure 8

There are disadvantages in this way of sitting. The right shoulder can easily push forward and the left shoulder back, thus twisting the instrument and the body to the left. This twists the back unnaturally. The twist is accentuated if the player turns further to the left to look at the fingerboard. It is easy for the front of the body to collapse and shorten, with rounding of the shoulders and more strain on the lower back. Dispensing with the footstool, and resting the guitar on top of a specially made cushion on the left leg is gaining popularity and acceptance. Using a footstool puts a strain on the lower back, which the use of the guitar cushion avoids.

One concert guitarist sits on a floor cushion in a semilotus posture. There is scope for freedom and experimentation. The best way to approach the question is to think what the body has to do to play the guitar, and how it might be best disposed to do it effectively and comfortably. As bodies vary greatly in size and shape, so will the solutions to this problem.

Good posture will involve keeping the body balanced and erect, without undue twisting or strain. In particular, it will involve keeping the head and neck free, with good primary control.

Faulty posture for a guitarist can lead to many difficulties, and some of these may seem far removed from anything to do with how the guitar is held. For example, it is possible to stabilize the guitar by pressing it towards the body with the right arm or wrist. This in turn pushes the right shoulder forward, and so twists the body backwards to the left again. This will cause backache. The resulting stiffness of the right hand will prevent the fingers from playing quickly and easily. They will tend to pull the strings up in free stroke, and the fingers will come out from, instead of into the hand. The hand will also tend to bounce upwards, away from the guitar. This will make the tone rather sharp and thin. The right hand finger action cannot be corrected on its own without reference to the whole posture. Instead of pushing the guitar inwards, the right arm must simply rest on top of it. The weight of the arm acting downwards and not pushing inwards is what stabilizes the guitar.

Another poor way to keep the guitar steady is to grip it with the left hand. This means that the thumb will curl round the fingerboard as if it were holding a violin. The fingers are pulled down and away from the strings, and the bass strings are out of reach. The palm of the hand is narrowed, restricting the movement of the fingers, so they have to jump from note to note, even if the notes are close together. Tension in the left shoulder can have the same effect, pulling the left hand back and down towards the ground, bringing the left forearm parallel to the floor. The result is playing which is neither smooth nor fluent. The remedy is to correct the posture.

Tension and Effort

Movement is most natural and effective when it is carried out with minimum effort, and this principle applies regardless of the size of the movement. A virtuoso musician or world-class athlete will nearly always give the impression that what they do is easy and effortless. In a sense it is, but we have not seen the time that has gone into building up that skill. In the hands of a master player, the guitar looks a simple instrument, an impression that is dispelled remarkably quickly by actually starting to learn it.

The line of least resistance is always the most effective, getting the greatest result for the least effort is an elegant and satisfying way of working. Learning and improving any skill involves becoming more sensitive and being able to detect smaller and smaller differences. For example, a good musician will know the exact lightness of touch, angle of fingers and degree of force to achieve the sound he wants. He has trained himself to be sensitive and smaller differences are significant to him. He can hear these same small differences in the playing of others. An artist is sensitive to shades of colour, and a wine taster must have a palate that makes very fine discriminations of taste. Learning a skill involves training in becoming more sensitive and being able to detect smaller significant differences in the chosen activity.

To become more sensitive, you must decrease the effort you make. Putting a lot of force into the fingers will never produce nuances of tone colour. Strain and pain are useless. The more force and effort, the less learning.

The Alexander Technique shifts the emphasis onto the way an action is performed rather than its end result. One immediate aspect of this is to focus attention on the amount of effort and muscular tension used by musicians to play their instrument.

It is difficult to accurately gauge how much muscle tension is needed to perform movements if they are habitual, or if all the attention is given to the end result. Too much effort may be used even in such simple actions as writing, or striking a guitar string.

Sometimes muscles are tense that have nothing directly to do with the task in hand. Clenching the jaw while playing is a good example from my own experience. This is a very common displacement of tension. Clenching the jaw does not actually help a performer to play any better, in fact, quite the opposite. There is research that suggests that jaw position has a real effect on hearing. A study by G. Schuchman and E. Burgi in 1971 showed that sensitivity to pure tones could be increased by moving the jaw bone. Threshold sensitivity could be increased on average by 15 decibels in this way. Moving the jaw position can increase the ability to hear. This is not really surprising, for hearing involves bones of the head being sensitive and free to transmit sound vibrations which are then interpreted by the brain. Fixing the bones of the jaw by clenching would be equivalent to putting the soft pedal on the piano and therefore damping the sound.

Apart from unnecessary tension, sometimes too many muscles are used to control an action. Which muscles to tense, and which to relax, and by how much is the critical question. It is important to discriminate as to the degree of effort needed, as well as which muscles to involve. One example is doing two different actions simultaneously, one with each hand. Putting more effort into one hand will usually make the other increase its effort in sympathy.

Playing loudly on the guitar with the right hand fingers will usually mean an unconscious and unnecessary increase in pressure by the left hand fingers on the strings. An even finer discrimination involves being able to play loudly with the right hand thumb, but keeping the right hand fingers playing softly. Eventually, independent control must be achieved over each right hand finger.

There is also the question of exactly which muscles to tense. Muscle fibres work on a binary principle. They are either on or off, relaxed or contracted. Complex movements by large muscles are built up by the relaxation or contraction of large numbers of different muscle fibres. Complete relaxation is as absurd as complete tension. Which muscles to tense or relax and by how much is the important question. Asking a student to 'relax' is not very useful. He will either collapse in a heap on the floor if he takes you literally, or feel even more tense, because your instructions are impossible to follow.

Lack of physical awareness can lead to tendinitis in instrumentalists. This is a painful inflammation of the tendons that control the fingers and it usually affects the wrist. It seems to be caused by trying to do two contradictory things at once, such as flexing a finger joint while at the same time unknowingly sending a message to make it contract. It is like driving a car while depressing the brake pedal.

Tendinitis can also be caused purely by excess muscular tension. I have a student who developed tendinitis in the wrist mainly from writing. When she writes, she uses so much force that she sometimes pushes the pen through the paper and tears it. Doing this for years finally forced the tendons in her wrist to lodge an emphatic protest which could not be ignored and this prevented her writing for some time.

Tendinitis is a crisis situation, but it does not come out of the blue. It is brought on by many years of faulty use, just as toothache is the ultimate result of years of dental neglect. Musicians have many occupational ailments: playing an instrument can put unusual stresses on the body, and even slight strains can build up through the years into painful conditions. One survey found that by the age of thirty, half the musicians questioned were suffering from some pain brought on by the muscular stresses of playing their chosen instrument (H. Fry 1986). The Alexander Technique can act as prevention as well as cure, and is important right from the start. Concentrating on the quality of an action; how it is carried out, prevents forming habits that could cause trouble later on.

Verbal Instructions

In the initial stages of learning, too many instructions confuse the issue and make students try to think of too many things at once. I think that most beginners will find a basically good guitar playing posture for themselves provided I guide them with a minimum of verbal instructions. The best way to reduce a student's posture to an uncomfortable shambles is to give him lots of verbal instructions on what not to do and correct him constantly. These suggestions may be right, but they are liable to have exactly the opposite effect to the one intended. If I tell someone not to bend his thumb, he has to access what this feels like; searching his experience in order to understand the instruction. Therefore such a direction is actually a command to think about bending the thumb and this will trigger the muscles to do it. It is like saying "Don't think of the colour blue!" In order to obey this instruction, you have to understand it, and in order to understand it you have to disobey it.

Verbal instructions must always be expressed positively: "Keep the thumb straight" rather than "Don't bend your thumb". This is a fundamental principle of good teaching.

Example and direct guidance are much better methods of bringing student and guitar together effectively. Our bodies learn remarkably well by watching and imitating examples using the kinaesthetic sense. This is much more effective than trying to remember something from a series of verbal instructions that are generated not from your own experience, but from someone else's. This is quite apart from the fact that the meaning you take from their words is bound to be distorted and incomplete. Guesswork is not too unkind a word for it. Words are on a different dimension to physical actions and can easily be misinterpreted to mean an action which was not intended. Remembering verbal instructions about how to sit (or worse, how not to sit) is nowhere near as effective as a proprioceptive memory of how it feels to sit well, which can then be reproduced at will.

The Alexander Technique works by actually giving the student the feeling of what it is like to act in a natural, unforced way. Natural movements are direct, fast, efficient, harmonious and satisfying. The Alexander Technique aims to re-educate the body to natural movements, paying particular attention to the primary control of the head and neck. A large part of the lesson is taken up with the Alexander teacher actually physically guiding the student to do straightforward actions, such as walking, or just sitting in a chair. Every time that action is carried out, it can be checked against the feeling of good balance and primary control. There is a Chinese saying "I hear and I forget. I see and I remember. I do and I understand."

Changing Technical Habits

A student will want to change a technical habit when he sees it is not getting the results he wants. Frustration will change habits, provided it does not lead to trying harder at the very thing that is not working.

Without this direct motive, changing technical habits is more difficult. For example, a student may press against the guitar with his right wrist. I will tell him not to and he may comply immediately, but it will go straight back to its habitual position as soon as his attention is distracted by something else. In order to stabilize the right hand, the whole posture will have to be adjusted, and with it his ideas of what is important in playing the guitar. I can see that his hand position is a barrier to free playing. A young student may see it differently. He may not have been playing for very long, and his last teacher may have been indifferent to this habit, or even recommended it. His hand feels comfortable there because it is a familiar position. He may not be aware of the tone he produces; so far so good, he thinks. Most important of all, he is playing music! This achievement is enough to cancel many imagined drawbacks. He knows that when he puts his hand in the funny (unfamiliar) position you have shown him, not only can he not play as well as he did before, but whenever he looks away it goes straight back to where it was, so it all seems pointless. A teacher needs good rapport with a student to persuade him to change for no immediate, discernible advantage. Adults are more likely to put aside immediate rewards (jam today) for more abstract advantages such as better technique (jam tomorrow), if you have convinced them there really will be jam tomorrow.

When Alexander was working with his voice problem, he would often give himself directions for his head to go forward and up, then would stop and do nothing further. In this position he could recite if he wished, but he did not decide in advance whether he would or not. Sometimes he would, but not always. This meant he was not distracted by the thought of having to recite, he kept a freedom of choice to the last minute. Continuously working in this way, he gradually changed his patterns of bodily use and was able to solve his voice problem. He found one of the greatest barriers to change was losing sight of the present. Concentrating on the end result would activate the very habits he was trying to change.

To take an illustration of this from my own experience, bending the thumb over the guitar fingerboard is a clear example of an ineffective way of playing. Many students do this in spite of (or because of?) being urged not to.

It is not enough simply to tell a student to repeat the music with the thumb straight. Like Alexander, the student may wish to keep the thumb straight and may even believe he is doing so, but the old habit will take over when he relaxes his attention. Bending the thumb has become part of playing the piece and has slipped out of conscious awarenesss. Trying not to bend it will have a very limited short term effect. A student will not actually want to bend it; this is a clear example of what Alexander realised. In order to do something about the thumb, you have to be aware of it. Then you have a choice. While you keep this awareness you have to be prepared for your musical performance to deteriorate, and not worry about mistakes. The end result, which is fluent playing, will come easily if the thumb is held in the most effective way. If you concentrate on keeping the thumb straight whatever you play, and not be concerned about the end product (the piece), then it will correct itself given time. This approach works for all habitual difficulties. Bending the thumb is likely to be too ingrained in the execution of known repertoire, so this difficulty is best dealt with by starting a completely new piece.

Another approach I sometimes use is to ask the student to deliberately bend the thumb. This has the same important effect, focusing his attention on the way he is playing. When something is in attention, it can no longer be an automatic habit. When I do this, a student will often realise for the first time just how uncomfortable it is to play this way. This will be a powerful force of change; he will remember his own discovery more readily than any outside exhortations.

I believe that being able to choose is better than having no alternative. So if a student is aware of bending the thumb and still chooses to do so, then the problem is on a totally different level; one of conscious disagreement, and both student and teacher know where they stand. The student will have to discover for himself how the hand works. I will still have confidence in my point of view and argue in favour of it.

I remember a particular lesson with a student who had a habit of letting her left hand fingers spring high off the strings when she played. I argued it was more effective if she kept them close to the strings. She disagreed, and I saw her getting ready for an argument. She said she could manage perfectly well as things were, and indeed she could for the moment. I am not sure she would buy my 'jam tomorrow' line. I might have persuaded her to try it, but it looked as though a battle was in prospect.

I tried a different approach. We talked about whether it would be a good thing to be able to control the fingers so that you could choose how to use them. We agreed this would be better than having no choice. Controlling the fingers you could let them spring up, or stay down at will, and really discover what worked and what did not. We agreed this would be useful. I pointed out that her fingers always sprang away whenever she played, so she lacked

this   control and choice. I said I was quite happy if her fingers sprang away from the strings provided she could also
keep them close if she wanted to. She smiled and agreed to
try for the control. I am sure she thought she had been
tricked somehow, (and maybe she was right), but it gave her
something useful to aim for: left hand finger control.

I could have been even more devious. I could have asked
her to bring her fingers up off the strings deliberately, and
so gain control of the involuntary movement from the opposite direction. Both approaches work equally well. Left at
the level of "This is better" ("No it isn't"), or "You do this"
("Oh no I won't"), we would have got nowhere.

I wonder why students often seem to pay no attention
to the signs and symbols in the music. These are
either fingering indications designed to make the piece
easier to play, or other signs denoting dynamics and
interpretation. If a student is having trouble with a passage,
the answer is often printed before his very eyes.

Students will often play a piece in a rather disjointed way
because they are not using the helpful fingering which is
clearly marked on the music. When I point this out, and ask
why they are not following the signs, they often say they are.
This is a very interesting answer. If the music is 'what' and
the fingering is 'how' to play, it seems to me they are
concerned with ·the end result (the 'what'), and have
developed a blind spot for the 'how'. This is another
parallel to Alexander's experiments, but much easier to
remedy. A little attention and they can use the fingering and
improve their performance.

I leave students free to disregard fingering if they want
to. However, they must see it, try it and think about it if
they are going to reject it. There are plenty of instances
where an alternative fingering may suit a player better.
These sort of directions need not be sacrosanct.

I think it is not very useful to talk about breaking habits.
Trying to break a habit is a waste of effort, because the very
word 'try' implies it is a difficult task. To quote Mark Twain,
"Giving up smoking is easy I do it every day". It is much
better to see habits clearly, to take them out of the stage of
unconscious   competence and to provide positive

alternatives. As long as an action is at the stage of unconscious competence it is unchangeable. It must be made conscious. Physical habits need physical experience to change them, not intellectual understanding. The purpose of a habit needs to be clearly defined and it will be accomplished by taking the right actions in the present.

Asking students to work against habit will actually hamper their playing ability initially. They will play worse. They are back at the stage of conscious competence, or even conscious incompetence. I will argue that later they will play better, but this may not be convincing at the time. So I am in the awkward position of purporting to improve their playing, while if they follow my instructions, they find they play worse! No wonder students resist. It must all come out into the open. Students do not want to handicap themselves, nor do they disregard what you say in order to annoy you (except very rarely!).

All habits bind the energy which went into repeating the action. They all have a specific technical purpose and an overall purpose, and so deserve some respect. For example, there is always a reason for a student bending his left hand thumb, or tensing his shoulders. The reason he does it must be to play the piece at all on the guitar. What other reason could there be?

It is possible to use this in a helpful way. Instead of concentrating on the negative aspect of the habit, it can be reframed to become an asset. The intention is positive, so the actual habit can be by-passed, and you can work with the intention. This basic desire to play the guitar better is a deep and powerful ally, if you can utilise it by going beyond the external (and contradictory) manifestation.

If I can find out a student's intention and get him to express it in a positive way, I can show him a better method of achieving it. We will be co-operating and not at odds with each other. Change will be easy and effortless.

I have been talking of habits and actions as if they are totally physical. Of course the reality is very much more complex. We strive for what we want and act to get it, driven by our thoughts and feelings. Our actions are these thoughts and emotions on a physical level.

I remember teaching a girl who was experiencing difficulty playing because she slumped forwards, angled the guitar outwards and flattened her right wrist, pushing the guitar inwards, to keep it steady. She was forced to play by pulling the strings upwards and she got a very poor tone. I had pointed this out and explained what was happening for some weeks. I asked her to bring her body up and over the guitar and adjust her head/neck/body balance. I also asked her to straighten the guitar and relax her right arm and wrist, but she was not changing.

At twelve years old, Gemma was at an age when she was acutely self-conscious of her body anyway. Looking back, I think she simply saw my observations as criticism and her refusal to change was a way of insisting that there was nothing wrong with her body despite her anxieties to the contrary.

One day I started to explain again, but stopped just in time as I saw her face was becoming flushed, and she was about to burst into tears. I rapidly changed the subject. I led the conversation round in a neutral way and apologised for nagging. I said this must have annoyed her and maybe she had got angry with me for not seeing her point of view. In the weeks that followed we established a better relationship, and she told me that she took my comments about her playing as criticism and did not understand what I was saying, despite nodding agreement to keep me quiet. We carried on working, and she started to improve her playing posture to a considerable extent. I was very slow to appreciate what Gemma was trying to tell me by her actions, and this probably added to her distress.

Our body is a very important part of our basic self-image, and ways of acting are inextricably bound up with, and expressive of, our emotions. Changing the way we use our body can release emotions into the open that have been previously connected with, and expressed by, physical habits. When I was having Alexander lessons, my teacher continually rearranged my body and asked me to do things, mundane things like sitting down, in a totally unfamiliar way. Intellectually, I understood perfectly well what she was doing, and why. I agreed with it. If I had not, I would have stopped the lessons. I felt extremely irritable before, during, and after these lessons, and I would get annoyed over trivial things. Changing my habitual ways of acting affected me emotionally.

The mind and body form a unity. Changing physical habits will change habitual thoughts; the Alexander Technique works from this direction. Changing thought processes will also affect physical habits; the two are complementary. Physical actions can be prepared, reinforced or changed by first rehearsing them mentally. This direction is of great interest to anyone who wishes to form habits and prepare actions in the most effective way with the least possible effort. I want to turn next to mental rehearsal in music.

Chapter Seven

Mental Rehearsal

When Alexander was formulating directions for his physical movements he would first imagine his body moving in the way he wanted; but not actually try to do it physically. For example, he would think of his head going forward and up, without actually doing it. He found this clarified his thoughts and prepared his body.

Thought does produce physical effects as it happens. Research has been done that shows clearly that thinking about particular muscle groups actually causes electrical discharges within them (Pelletier 1979). Electrochemical charges are generated and can be measured by electromyographic (EMG) readings. Physiologically, the neural pathways used when imagining an action are the same as those used when actually performing it.

This relationship of mind and body is fascinating and opens up very interesting possibilities for mentally rehearsing skills without the actual physical movements. Various studies have shown that a combination of mental and physical rehearsal is at least as good as, or better than, physical practice only (Magill 1980, Richardson 1967).

Mental rehearsal has been used in sport, drama and music to enhance performance. Psychologist Richard Suinn of Colorado State University has trained Olympic athletes in a method he calls 'Visio - motor behaviour rehearsal' (Suinn 1976). This involved athletes in a programme of progressive relaxation followed by muscular and visual imagery of their sport before they actually engaged in it. During these experiments, Suinn recorded EMG readings of a skier as he visualised a downhill run, and noted the electrical readings of various muscles. These EMG recordings were almost identical to those obtained on the course itself. There was a final burst of muscle activity after the subject imagined himself passing the finishing line. This seemed odd until someone pointed out it is impossible to come to an instantaneous stop from 40 mph.

There is other research which worked with free throws in basket ball (D. Lauck 1978). The only team to improve its percentage of hits from the initial to the final trial was a team using a combination of relaxation and visualization. Curiously enough, the teams that actually kept throwing got worse. Similar methods of training athletes are used all over the world.

In both examples, a method of relaxation was used, developed by Edmund Jacobsen at Harvard University. It is based on systematically tensing and relaxing various muscle groups and learning to attend to and discriminate between the resulting sensations (Jacobsen 1964). It has some features in common with the Alexander Technique.

There is an interesting musical study of mental rehearsal. A very experienced conductor, who also believed himself to be a strong internal visualiser was asked to imagine himself conducting the Overture to *Die Fledermaus* by Johann Strauss. EMG readings were taken when he was actually conducting the piece, when he mentally rehearsed conducting to taped music, and when he mentally rehearsed conducting from the score. Readings were also taken while he was mentally hearing the music from the score. All the conditions saw an increase in EMG readings from a baseline state. Apart from when he was actually conducting, the greatest increase occurred when he was mentally conducting from taped music.

The EMG readings for mental rehearsal were less than those obtained from an actual physical peformance, but both showed the same profile: they closely followed the shape of the music as it changed texture, rhythm and dynamics. There was an increase in the EMG readings for the first twelve bars (Allegretto Vivace), followed by a decrease in the subsequent reflective, slower passage.

The muscle activity in mental rehearsal closely corresponded to the mood of the music throughout. It increased particularly at the end of the movement where the music becomes louder, faster, and more densely orchestrated (Evelyn I. Bird 1985).

Submodalities

Mental rehearsal creates and reinforces the internal kinaesthetic, visual and auditory parts of the performance. This in turn prepares the muscles for the actual physical movements and clarifies the performer's task both technically and musically.

Studies of mental rehearsal tend to concentrate on visualization. Even with such an imprecise approach however, results are still very impressive. It is possible using representational systems to go into much greater detail and create a unique way to suit each individual, for everyone uses their senses in a unique way.

So far, I have discussed the internal senses in fairly general terms, but each person makes characteristic distinctions within them. These distinctions are known as submodalities, and are the smallest components in the structure of subjective experience.

Picture yourself as clearly as possible in a pleasant experience. Are you inside the picture (associated), or looking on at yourself having that experience (dissociated)? Is the picture in colour or is it black and white? Is it a moving film, or still frames? These are three of the most important visual distinctions. They do not refer to the content of the picture, only to the way it is seen.

Now take time to hear the sounds in your imagined experience. How loud is the sound that you are hearing? Can you turn the volume up? Does it emanate from any particular point? Do you add a kinaesthetic element to your experience? Is there a sense of weight? Of temperature? Of pressure? Where do you feel it?

We habitually recreate and imagine our experience in different ways and it is clear that the quality of our memories, daydreams, hopes and fears can be radically altered by changing the submodalities of the internal senses.

SUBMODALITIES

Visual
Associated or dissociated (seen through own eyes, or looking on at self)
Colour or black and white
Location of picture (eg left or right, up or down)
Distance of picture
Brightness
Contrast
Clarity (blurred or focused)
Movement (film or slide show)
Speed (faster or slower than normal)
Number (split screen or multiple images)
Panorama or framed

Auditory
Volume (loud or soft)
Tone (soft or harsh)
Timbre (full or thin)
Location of sound
Distance (how far away)
Stereo or mono
Duration
Speed (faster or slower than normal)
Clarity

Kinaesthetic
Location
Intensity
Pressure (hard or soft)
Extent
Texture
Weight

This list of submodalities is not meant to be exhaustive; it shows only the main distinctions. Most are enshrined in linguistic metaphors, giving a literal representation of the speaker's inner world of thought.

It is worth finding out your critical submodalities and

whether changing them changes the quality of your memories. Take some time to remember and picture an ordinary experience. If it is associated, step outside it. If it is dissociated, step into it and see if this makes a difference. Make it brighter, now darker. If it is in colour, try it in black and white or vice versa. Bring it right up close. Now push it further and further away. You are controller of your own personal picture show, the master of your internal world. These changes will change the quality of the experience. For most people a bright, close, associated picture is most effective. This has nothing to do with the truth or falsity of memory. Nothing will change the actual event in the past, but the memory of that event can be changed to give it a different meaning and associated feeling.

You can also manipulate your own personal internal stereo system in the auditory mode. Make the sound louder or softer, slow the sound or speed it up. Make changes in the kinaesthetic modality. Make the feeling hard or soft, rough or smooth. Some of these changes may make it more pleasant; some will make it less pleasant. By manipulating submodalities it is possible to neutralize painful memories and enhance pleasant ones.

This is a matter of sense experience; difficult to convey with words. Once you actually experience your own characteristic ways of thinking, it means more than any amount of theory, which may or may not be true. Theory is arguable, experience is convincing. The only way to find out if ideas are useful is to try them out. You do not have to decide if they are true or false, you can use those that interest you. Inertia is the great enemy of change, especially if what you are doing already is enjoyable and successful. There are many chances to make it more enjoyable and more successful! Pleasure and fulfilment need not be limited. Absolutely the only limitations to success and enjoyment exist in our own minds, not in the external world.

Experience what happens when you match predicates and mirror gestures, tonality and breathing. It can be done in any relationship. You will not be able to do this all at once: the learning process is the same as for any complex skill. You start by mastering a small chunk, then adding others until the end result is unimaginably complicated compared to the starting point. It is also valuable to see what happens when you consistently mismatch predicates, gestures, tonality and breathing.

See, hear and feel the results when you use the Meta Model to be precise about a student's difficulties. Hear the responses to the questions. Systematically notice body language, breathing changes and lateral eye movements. There is a fantastic wealth of information all around that we are blind, deaf and numb to nearly all the time. The world is infinitely richer than we can ever imagine. Find out your own preferred and lead representational systems and those of the people around you. Find out your own critical submodalities within them by experimenting and changing them. Play, experiment and improvise. This makes everything so enjoyable. We owe it to our students to do so, if any justification were needed.

In workshops and seminars we use submodality patterns to explore feelings such as stage fright. Stage fright is a mixture of many different ideas and feelings, but there is usually a picture of failure involved. This picture is false. Fear stands for False Expectations About Reality. If I am going to create pictures of the future, they might as well be pleasant ones. I find it impossible to be frightened of any performing situation if I take the picture of failure that I am creating, shrink it to a quarter size, push it away, bleach it of colour and add ridiculous circus music in the background. It becomes ludicrous instead of frightening.

Mental Rehearsal for Improvement

Mental rehearsal works on the internal systems without the actual external playing. I think that by making these secure, the actual performance is made more secure.

Firstly, a method of relaxation seems to enhance the performer's ability to visualise clearly. The feeling of relaxation is difficult to define, but freedom from anxiety is important. Any anxiety about success or failure is liable to be distracting and interfere with mental rehearsal, just as it does in an actual performance. However the Jacobsen method of relaxation also involves discrimination in muscle use, and this is an essential element.

I think practice of the Alexander Technique would be more useful and specific than any ill-defined relaxation, which is likely to mean ten different things to ten different individuals. Firstly, the Alexander Technique can be used to put the body into a comfortable position, either lying down, or sitting with the instrument as if about to play. Secondly, mentally rehearsing good use of muscles is likely to be more effective than mentally rehearsing habitually poor use of muscles. It will build up a better internal kinaesthetic check. This would be obvious if the action was being done for real.

Good use of muscles would be most important when slowly mentally rehearsing technical exercises, when you need to be very clear which muscles to move. The internal kinaesthetic feeling would be less important when mentally rehearsing whole pieces. Here, technique would be taken for granted, just as it is in reality. Continuity and interpretation would be paramount.

Playing a musical instrument involves very fine motor discrimination and mental rehearsal can be used for small muscle movements of the hands in technical exercises, full scale performances and anything between these extremes. Mental rehearsal does not yet seem to have been systematically applied to the first few years of instrumental learning, but it can be used at any point in learning music, to reinforce the specific internal kinaesthetic, auditory and visual representations of a particular piece.

I began with Alexander's idea of direction: simply thinking of the movement, but not actually doing it. However, most discussions of mental rehearsal have focused on visualization: actually making pictures of yourself playing. This emphasis on visualization is a weakness. Not everyone can lead into internal fantasies by visualising, nor is visualization the most important part of mental rehearsal. Some students might find it easiest to lead kinaesthetically, others auditorily. And both these aspects are musically more important than the visual one. First establish the student's lead representational system and use that to start the mental rehearsal. A teacher who uses only one method is likely to be operating out of his own lead and dominant systems and generalising about everyone else.

Having established the best way to lead into mental rehearsal, the next step is to find out which submodalities are the most important for the student. This can be done by asking her to imagine a pleasant experience, the actual situation does not matter, nor do you need to know exactly what it is. Then, ask her to vary systematically the submodalities of the experience one at a time in each system, seeing, hearing and feeling which ones make the most difference. Some will make the experience more vivid, pleasant and distinct. Others will make it less so. The visual submodalities usually have the most impact (if I can mix a metaphor).

Once the critical submodalities are established, make sure the student uses them. Have her make a big, close, bright picture, if these are what will give her experience most emphasis. Mental rehearsal must be done with an associated picture. The kinaesthetic aspect (the feel of playing the instrument) cannot be created without this.

I would get a student who leads visually to create a picture of herself ready to play, with the music in front of her. If she finds this difficult, she may find looking upwards is a help. I would ask her to make sure she is inside this picture, and to make it as clear as she can using her important submodalities. Then I would ask her to feel her fingers on the guitar. When she can do this, she can add the sounds and start playing the piece in her imagination. Her mental rehearsal is now at full strength. This sequence is the most useful for many students. With some, it may be better to start from the kinaesthetic feel of the instrument, and then overlap to the visual and auditory. With others, mentally hearing the piece first might facilitate the picture and the feelings.

It is not always possible to do all of this at once. Students may need some weeks to familiarise themselves with the internal use of their senses and to take the fullest advantage of them. They may well need to work on their ability to hear a piece internally. The most important point is to be alert and guided by the student's experience, what she tells you verbally and non-verbally.

Mental Rehearsal for Memorization

Memorizing a piece means forming reliable internal auditory, visual and kinaesthetic representations. These can be formed and reinforced without actually playing. A piece is truly memorized when the performer can write it out from memory and mentally rehearse it complete with left and right hand fingering, hearing the sound mentally as he does so.

Memorizing uses the same process as mental rehearsal for improvement. It is easiest for most people to start by visualising playing the piece, with an associated image. Then they can overlap to the other senses and use their submodalities. Once in the picture, feel the sensations of actually playing, the finger movements, posture and breathing involved and then add the soundtrack. Sound is not so important in sport, but it is the whole essence of music.

Discriminating muscle memory, and the ability to start from anywhere in the piece, must be allied with a clear auditory memory and some picture of the music. An understanding of the underlying structure and harmony is also important. Some musicians have a very strong eidetic memory and can picture the score in their minds and then play from it as if it were really on the music stand in front of them. Even with this talent, a combination of senses works best and relying on any one can lead to disaster under pressure. Relying too much on muscle memory is dangerous, it depends on continuity, one movement preparing the next. If something goes wrong, the piece will stop immediately and have to start again from the beginning. Under stress in a performance, muscle memory can easily break down unless backed up by other methods.

Too much reliance on visualization is dangerous too. A sudden or unexpected movement can literally knock the picture out of one's mind, and once again the piece will break down. Setting too much store on aural memory has the danger that a sudden noise will break the thread of the piece and the performer will lose his place.

Performers are usually strong in one area and neglect the others. Many problems students experience with memorizing can be solved by working with the internal senses. Many people do not know how they think, which systems they use, or in which order they use them. Internal senses can be strengthened by conscious use. Nearly everyone has the possibility of using all three internal senses, only habit prevents them. We all have more resources than we actually use. I have improved students' musical memory simply by working with them on visualization.

Some performers work on a piece of music mentally for some time before they actually play a note of it on their instrument. Using the submodalities can make this process even more effective. Mental rehearsal gives the performer responsibility for his own playing and uses the right hemisphere of the brain. Any fuzzy areas in the internal visualising, feeling and hearing of the music will show where the piece is insecure. Mental rehearsal cannot substitute for actual playing, but it does clarify the music by creating it away from the instrument. Otherwise the actual 'hands-on' playing will only reflect the muddle and inconsistencies of the way it has been learned. It is another useful choice for teachers and performers to improve their own playing and the playing of their students.

Chapter Eight

Permission to be Wrong

The idea of a "teacher teaching a student" is a linguistic straightjacket on any enjoyable progress in a music lesson and restricts what both participants can learn. The phrase suggests that the teacher is the active party passing information and skill to the student, the receiver. The teacher therefore has the answers and the student is there to obtain them. The more this becomes the lesson model, the more helpless the student will feel and the more burdened down with responsibility the teacher will become. All the student can do is to measure his own inadequacy against pre-existing standards and such lessons can easily degenerate into weekly reminders to students of how badly they play and how they keep making the same mistakes, despite being constantly corrected. Even if you are careful to avoid this approach, students may think this anyway, despite reassurances; you are just being "nice". The important fact is what they actually perceive, regardless of your intention.

To believe in this destructive model of learning will make it a reality. Instead, students actively make their own meaning of what you say in their own way. The more they can develop their own talents and capabilities, the more confident and competent they will become and the more they will be able to direct their own learning.

I sometimes underestimate my students' talents and so they often surprise me. They need me not so much to tell them what to do, but to give them permission to use the knowledge and resources they already have. Students can often correct their own mistakes with very little direct help. Hesitant and uncertain playing will become confident and rhythmic with the minimum of suggestions or instructions from me. Sometimes my interfering and asking questions actually inhibits their performance. Students already have all the resources they need. I try not to feel that I am there to give them something they lack.

Giving students permission to go wrong avoids this self-defeating view of lessons. They need to relax from the tyrannical compulsion of trying to get things "right". Striving for excellence is a positive force for improvement, but the negative aspect of avoiding mistakes can stifle learning, experimentation, fun and curiosity. Permission to fail takes away the cycle of fault and blame. To get something "wrong", or not to know information, does not make you a stupid person, it simply means you were not correct on one particular occasion. From the point of view of the total learning process, a mistake might be extremely useful.

Students need permission to praise what was right and to acknowledge and build on positive virtues in technique or performance. I always ask what went right about a performance; what they were satisfied with. They need permission to go wrong. Without this they will be reluctant to take risks and so will not actually play as well as they can. It is like walking along a path two feet wide: hardly likely to cause careful and circumspect movements. But if this path was over a deep ravine! Walking the path now would be a very different matter, yet it is only the focus of attention that has changed, not the path or your bodily co-ordination.

Focus on failure hampers performance and creativity. Many times I feel students are half-hearted in what they do, not willing to take risks or experiment for fear of making a mistake. This actually makes them more prone to errors than if they were in a relaxed, confident frame of mind. Fear of failure will actually generate mistakes by making students anxious rather than interested.

The best performances are done carelessly. The skills are second nature, music is played without a care and this joyful feeling will be communicated to any audience. It is not done carelessly in the sense of not caring. The musician will care very deeply about what he does.

Permission to go wrong does not mean being indifferent to what happens, or that one answer is as good as another and that all ways of playing are equal. A time signature of four over four means four crotchets in a bar and always will, unless musicians change the rules, and if a student wishes to enter the world of music, he must know this. In the same way, pushing the right hand inwards so that the wrist is flattened and touches the front of the guitar is less effective than having the wrist relaxed outwards. Pitches and rhythms are clearly and exactly specified in most music and must be played as written. What is destructive to learning is concentrating on what can go wrong and trying to avoid it, and taking the attitude that a lesson is a place where mistakes are made for the teacher to correct; so justifying his existence, and giving him something to do. The better the teacher of course, the more subtle mistakes he can see.

Students need permission not to know answers to questions. Much information is straightforward. A filled-in note with a stem is called a crotchet. The sixth string of the guitar sounds the note of E. However, factual replies rely on an understanding of music or the instrument: they connect with other facts and skills. Sometimes even understanding the question is a problem: young students may know the information from another context, but find it difficult to transfer it to the present one. It is also quite possible to learn facts without understanding them or connecting them together in any way.

If students see themselves as helpless and learning as being told what to do, then lessons can take the following possible forms. Firstly, the learner can strive for the answer. Secondly, the teacher can tell the student in a straight transfer of information. Thirdly, the student may try to force or trick the teacher into telling him what the answer is. Lessons can then degenerate into more and more devious attempts by the student to get the answer if the teacher will not tell him immediately. One good way of doing this is by continually making a mistake. A teacher can stir up some very interesting consequences if he refuses to give an answer, assuming he knows it, whatever happens. I thoroughly recommend this experiment to all teachers. It is best to answer a question immediately, or not at all. Trying to coax the answer out of a student does not work very well.

Socrates and Guesswork

I used the Socratic Method of teaching a great deal in
the past. The theory of this approach sounds convincing
but the reality is disappointing. The idea is that the
student will discover within himself knowledge and
understanding if the teacher asks leading questions;
these help the student to think in the right direction, and
to come up with the answer without being told. Sometimes this works as planned, but more recently, I have become rather discouraged with it as a way of teaching.

What happens is that the student usually assumes that
you are leading to the right answer in a roundabout way.
So he tries to get it with an inspired combination of intui-
tion and guesswork, reading clues from your questions,
manner and tone of voice. This reminds me of a psychic
reading by a fortune teller at a fairground. It starts with a
few general observations, and if the line seems encourag-
ing, more specific ones, until with your help, your area
of interest (which you wanted to hear about in the first
place) has been pinpointed. So all the student has to do is
sit back and you are bound to tell him in the end anyway.
The Socratic Method will not work in an environment
where the emphasis is on getting a predetermined right
answer to satisfy those in authority.

I was always aware that children guess answers. Sometimes they are lucky and their guess is correct, but this
leads only to a dead end. A correct guess is worse than a
wrong one, because it gives the impression of understanding. Recently I have become more aware, and have been
surprised by how much guesswork goes on, it is much
worse than I thought. I would estimate about three quarters
of the answers are guesses.

If you know the answer to a question, you will give it. If
you do not, the most constructive thing to do is to say so.
However, one common teaching approach seems to demand some answer, any answer, to satisfy the questioner
and so students become fortune tellers. Most teachers
have experienced giving an explanation, and thinking the
student has clearly understood it because he answers

correctly. A week later however, it becomes obvious that he does not know at all. Guesswork is the culprit. The right answer to satisfy the teacher at the time has become a substitute for understanding.

It is difficult to admit to not knowing or understanding. Hard for both student and teacher. Sometimes the only honest reply to a question is "I don't know". This is an exciting starting point, not an admission of failure and it is the only response that allows for progress. To get a child to admit that he does not know the answer to a question is extremely difficult. Children tend to guess if they do not know, or sit in thoughtful silence, looking as if they are searching for the answer. This is an unhappy situation, but a direct result of an educational ethos that wants right answers, or failing that, any answer. In fact being willing not to know is the key to discovery. As long as you think you have got the right answer, you are unlikely to discover anything new.

Witting and Unwitting Answers

Knowledge about musical facts may be simple, but playing an instrument is not. There are many possibilities for error; wrong notes, wrong timing, poor technical habits, to name but a few. The player has to use many skills at once - some will still be at the stage of conscious incompetence.

If a student does make a mistake, the first thing to establish is does he know it? If it was a wrong note, did he mean to play it? If he did not, what went wrong? An isolated slip? The right hand on the wrong string perhaps, or the left hand in the wrong place. Suppose he did mean to play it. He may have misread the note, or thought it was located on the guitar in a different place to its actual fret.

Rhythmic mistakes are much more difficult to pinpoint. He may be unclear about note values, or the pulse may be wayward. Very often the difficulty of moving the left hand to a particular note or chord will cause a hesitation. In this case, it is not really a timing mistake at all, but a technical one, corrected by analysing the left hand change and increasing the speed and accuracy of the finger movements.

I found that students nearly always have the idea that they are wrong when I ask about timing mistakes in lessons, although they may not know specifically how to do it right. They may not say anything at all about it unless you ask them.

Many students have difficulty with rhythm. I remember working with one on the melody of a Catalan folk song, 'El Noy de la Mare'. This piece has a recurring rhythm of dotted crotchet followed by quaver. He would play it either as equal crotchets, or with a shortened quaver.

In the past, I might have tackled this in a number of ways. Perhaps with a metronome. Maybe a demonstration and full-scale explanation complete with a diagram of how long the different notes last relative to each other. However this time I thought I would try something else. As he looked unhappy, I stopped him and asked what was wrong.

"These dotted notes are too short, and the quavers are too long," he said. "My timing is terrible. I really should count, but I never can."

"OK" I said, "If that's what you think, make the dotted crotchet longer and the quaver shorter, and see how that turns out."

He went ahead and played it again, more accurately.

"How was that?" I said. "Better." He replied, "But I'm still rushing the dotted crotchet."

"Try it again and see how it turns out if you make it longer still." I never said he was right (or wrong), and I did not say exactly how much longer it should be.

He played it again, this time correctly and what was more, he knew it was correct. I wondered what I had done to help him. Really nothing at all! I had only given him a chance to use his own power, he could become for a moment his own teacher. I wondered why he did not do it in the first place. He had all the resources he needed already.

I think he played it correctly because I was not putting pressure on him to get it "right" and he could connect the music with his own sense of rhythm. My instructions were so vague, he could hardly go wrong. I managed to reverse the usual situation. Before this, he was trying so hard to be right that his attention was on the possibility of making a mistake, and he duly made it. He assumed he did not really know what was right, but I did, and so relied on me to tell him. Having permission to be wrong is a release to find what is actually there without being distracted by anxiety or pressure. Getting the timing right was certainly his goal, and mine too, but above and beyond this, my overall teaching purpose was for him to gain confidence and competence in music.

Experimentation

Once you dispense with the idea of trying to elicit right answers, there is room for experimentation and discovery. Guessing and experimenting are quite different. Guessing is knowing that you do not know a required answer, but feeling obliged to say something anyway; you are caught in the right answer trap. As your answer is quite haphazard, being right is an unlooked-for bonus. Experimentation is based on the question "What happens if.....?" and its purpose is to find out more information about an idea or a process. Thinking in terms of right or wrong guesses is useless as far as learning is concerned. It closes the door to further knowledge. Experiments give worthwhile knowledge whatever happens. There is no such thing as a wrong answer in a scientific experiment - if scientists had taken that attitude we would still be believing that the sun went round the earth. There is no failure, only feedback. The "Scientific Method" can be applied to any branch of human knowledge. The Arts and the Sciences are only different in content and the same process of discovery can be applied to both.

Experimentation is a powerful way of learning and young children are great scientists; so much of the world is unfamiliar to them. A music student of any age is also dealing with a largely unfamiliar world and an experimental approach can be just as effective. When I see small children I see innocence and curiosity at their height.

I remember my daughter at the age of two and a half putting keys in the locks of various doors. She was not able to open them every time, but she liked to fit the keys in all the same, and did so from an early age. Initially I told her the correct key, but this spoiled the game; she liked to try every key on my key ring in the lock. I let her know which way up the key went, but she still experimented by inserting them upside down. When she tried the wrong key of course it did not fit. Nor did the right key fit if it was upside down. However it was as interesting for her to see what happened when she put the key in upside down as when she put it in correctly. She needed to discover for herself; she did not know already, whereas I did.

When she put the key in upside down it did not fit. Excellent! That confirmed her hypothesis about the key. She tried another key. Good. It did not fit either. She suspected as much. These experiments told her more about the nature of keys and locks, how they work, and how they are constructed, than using the right key to open the door. In fact fitting the right key cannot tell you very much about locks and keys at all. The right key is fine if you need to get inside the house quickly, and an adult who knows about locks would not use any other. As my daughter was more interested in finding out, the right one was the least interesting. Extending the analogy, the teacher knows an answer, but for the learner, discovering more about music and the process of playing is more important.

Trying

"Try" is a word that crops up in lessons all the time. I find myself saying to students "Try it again", when they have made a mistake, and "Do it again", when they have done it once successfully. "Try" seems to be a word rather like "Practice", perfectly harmless on the surface, but with hidden implications that can twist it into the opposite of its original meaning.

My dictionary defines the word "try" as "Test the qualities of (person or thing) by experiment......." Yet to think of somebody trying to do something tends to conjure up visions of him straining in vain at an inherently difficult task. It is almost synonymous with difficulty and anxiety. When I ask a student to do some musical task during the week and he says "I'll try", I find this very often means either he will not, or does not really want to, so his efforts will be half-hearted, or he does not really expect to be able to do it. Yet to try to do something in the dictionary sense need not have any association with hard labour, or even success and failure, as I "try" to make clear to my students.

The phrase "trying harder" is a contradiction. Scientists do not "experiment harder" if they do not get the answers they want. They may invest more time on the problem, but that is a different matter. They use the results as feedback and change their expectations, or the experiment. I think "trying harder" is code for doing more of the same (unsuccessful) thing you have already done. It has not worked so far, or you would not be contemplating doing it "harder", so more of the same is unlikely to make any difference. If you always do what you've always done, you'll always get what you've always got. If you cannot do something, then select another method, to see if it will achieve the results you wish. Trying harder is a dead end, because it ignores feedback and implies difficulty. It is a phrase I leave outside the classroom door where the modal operators can keep it company.

Overteaching

Overteaching is the teacher "trying harder"; at best it is a lot more work than necessary. Most, if not all teaching difficulties stem from not taking the student's way of learning into account. He may see the light, it may click with him, or he may be able to grasp it if it is presented another way, in accord with how he sees, hears and feels.

Very often teachers do talk too much, using a large part of the lesson to explain something very elegantly, but the time would be better spent with the students doing it for themselves. Overteaching is taken as normal. More valuable information comes from doing something than from listening to someone talk about it. On many occasions I have noticed that if I refrain from constantly correcting a student, his playing will improve. Simply asking him to repeat the phrase several times without any pressure to get it right will often eliminate the mistakes. It is possible to get too concerned about teaching a skill and feel a failure if the student does not understand, or improve by the end of a lesson. This is falling into the trap of taking the short view. Most learning and change is at an unconscious level anyway, so the point might be understood later with no more effort needed on the teacher's part.

Using a vocabulary that the student understands makes lessons easier too. When I used words in my explanations which my younger students did not understand, they would rarely say so. It is difficult for children to tell a teacher they do not understand. They feel stupid. Children are led to assume teachers are always right, and they should understand what they are taught - if they do not, it is their own fault. Also they are not exactly sure of what they know, or how your explanation fits into their body of knowledge. They nod sagely and hope that they will pick it up as they go along.

I think overteaching is also an attempt to transfer our understanding of a point to a student wholesale. "My knowledge" is not the same as "my car". It is only "mine" when I understand, connect and integrate it with my previous thoughts and experiences, so it cannot be transferred as if it were material. Facts can be taught but not understanding, and facts are meaningless unless connected with others in a coherent body of knowledge. The important target in teaching is how the student learns. Understanding cannot be transferred, split, taken or refused. Its very existence depends on the person who has it. This was vividly brought home to me when a friend explained at great length how understanding and experience cannot be made concrete and passed on from one person to another. He worked very hard to give me that insight; as if it were something material! I understood only when I saw how his method of explanation had failed to make me understand.

It was a superb recursive demonstration on his part; it may even have been deliberate.

Hit and Miss

It takes a long time to work against the 'Rule of the Right Answer', especially in schools. Students come from the last lesson and stay in the same frame of mind. The content of the lesson may have changed, but surely the teacher must still want all the right answers. Schools seem to want right answers, not curiosity and experimentation. In doing so, they reflect a general social attitude. Yet lessons can provide consistent experiences that curiosity and experimentation are valuable in themselves and a most effective way of learning.

I use experimentation when working on left hand position changes on the guitar. To change position smoothly involves a quick co-ordinated movement that often has to be done without looking. Experienced players will have built up the internal kinaesthetic 'feel' for the fingerboard and use this to make jumps smooth and accurate without having to look.

Missing a position change by a whole fret will get a wrong note. Missing by a smaller amount will make the note rattle unpleasantly. When this happens, the guitarist may curse, classify it as a failure, and try again without paying any further attention to it. In fact that miss is just as useful as a hit. It gives the body information about how it feels to hit the wrong fret. By paying attention to what happens, we know what it is like to miss. This feeling can then be used as feedback to adjust future efforts.

We learn by feedback so it is a waste to reject information before we start. Learning is not a 'hit or miss', but a 'hit and miss' affair. Learning by feedback and paying attention to what we do is more economical; a miss is not a 'failure', and we have a method of approaching any position change and not just the specific one being worked on at the time. Of course in a concert we want to hit the right fret, but learning how to do it is a different process.

I was teaching an advanced student who was struggling with a bar in the fifth Prelude by Villa-Lobos involving a shift from the second to the seventh fret. She was playing in position two; her first finger was pressed down on the second fret and she had to move her hand quickly and smoothly to press her first finger down on fret seven without looking.

Gill was missing regularly, becoming annoyed with herself and apprehensive that I too would become annoyed at her 'failure'. Firstly I asked her to spread her left hand so that in second position her fourth finger was hovering over fret five without actually touching it. This gave her a kinaesthetic marker for fret five that was only two frets away from her final destination (fret seven). She now had to judge a distance of only two frets instead of the original five. This is a good straightforward way of making shifts easier on the guitar, and her success rate improved considerably.

Next she experimented with the shift to see where it landed. I asked her to deliberately miss, first by going one fret too far, then by going one fret too low. I asked her each time to imagine the sound she would get as she did it, and match the feeling sense to the aural.

Paradoxically, by missing, she increased her sense of mastery, for if you know how to miss a target, you must know where it is, and how to hit it. Her left hand shift became secure. Any action you can reproduce at will must be under your control. You can have confidence in it and use it whenever you wish. If you can gain control of a mistake, you can choose whether to make it or not.

Musical Homeopathy

If a student or a group complains about some musical or technical difficulty, asking them consciously to exaggerate it allows them to take control and change it. What was a mistake, is now a positive virtue. Many students who have felt they were playing pieces lifelessly, brought them to life when asked to play as lifelessly as possible. It is well worth trying. But what if the result is an even more lifeless performance? Then by doing this they have demonstrated a conscious control over that element they were complaining about. After all, if they can make it more lifeless, they must also be able to make it less so. Either way, they are no longer helpless. Either way they (I almost wrote I) win.

I taught a guitar ensemble regularly for about two years. One week we were working on an arrangement of a quartet by Palestrina. The music was quite simple: crotchets and minims in common time, but when they played the first eight bars, the timing was completely out. I tried many ways to improve it, including a lot of repetition, but the result was not much better. I could not understand why they could not play such simple music in time.

I asked them to play the right notes, but in free time. This worked quite well; there was permission to get the time wrong, and we started to enjoy ourselves. Shoulders opened up, jaws unclenched. Then we played any note, but in the written time. More relaxation. The result was a quasi-Schoenberg atonal melody. We were enjoying ourselves at last.

Next I asked everyone to concentrate on the sound they were making. This is one of the best ways of clarifying ensemble music. Soon the tone was very much better. They had permission to go wrong as long as they listened to the sound. The ensemble had improved, but was still not completely together. I asked for suggestions from the group. (Why should I think of all the ideas?)

"Let's try it faster; it's difficult to keep time at such a slow speed."

"Can we tap our feet to the beat as we play it?"

"Can you count out loud for us?"

We did all these, and other things too, but with only partial success. There were complaints that this was a boring piece, and I felt that this was a fair comment. There was little rhythmic variety and everyone was losing interest. I did think the piece had something to offer if we could only see it in a fresh light. We had yet to hear it with the right notes, in time, played with the best possible tone. Finally, as they had complained that it was boring, I "prescribed the symptom", and asked them to play it bor-

ingly. I asked them to bore me to tears with it and send me
to sleep if they could. At last we had a lovely performance-
correct notes in time and a good tone. The music had come
alive. The group heard it too, and, for the first time, said
they actually liked the piece. We had finally managed to
by-pass concern about accuracy and actually achieved what
we were aiming for in the first place, by doing the opposite.

This musical homeopathy leads to some interesting discoveries. One advanced student was playing a Fantasia by
John Dowland. Whenever she began a particular phrase,
she always did a double-take. She would play the first note,
hesitate slightly, then start again and play it faultlessly.

I pointed this out, and of course she knew she was
doing it, and said she could not help it, it was now too
habitual. She said she would have to relearn the passage
very slowly from the beginning to eliminate the
hesitation. What she said was true, but I thought I would
try another, possibly quicker way through the difficulty.

I asked her what would happen if she did not pause. She
thought for a moment and said she was not sure, but
would probably make a mistake. I asked her to force
herself to play without stopping, because we needed to
discover what she was trying to avoid. Julie did so, and
made a left hand slip. This was the mistake she was
trying not to make by pausing. Now she knew what it
was, she could put it right in about five seconds, and play
the phrase through without stopping. She was trying to
avoid the finger slip, but in doing so had broken the musical continuity, and forgotten exactly what she was trying
to avoid.

To focus attention on an action will change it. Directing
students' attention on what they are doing forces a change.
Their playing now has an extra dimension and it is
impossible for them to play the piece in the same way as
before. They can no longer use the same (unsatisfactory)
strategy they had been using previously when they
were not paying attention. The key to teaching and
learning is where to place your attention. The most valuable and lasting learning involves a change in perception.

I have used this same approach with many students. I

remember a particular student who was studying a piece by the Spanish composer, Joaquim Rodrigo. He was playing extremely well, and his technical control of the piece was very good. Before taking a closer look at interpretation, I asked him if there were any particular improvements he would like to make.

"Yes," he said. "I don't think I play with enough feeling. I play it in a way that seems too dry and academic."

This made me stop and think. I would never have thought of this myself; it was a very personal observation. Clearly he felt something was lacking. There are many ways to explore this, perhaps by visualization, or by musical analysis of phrases, or seeing what images are conjured up by the music in a guided fantasy. I chose first to ask him to play it to me as mechanically as possible.

He gave me a strange look and proceeded to play the piece according to instructions. It was a very mechanical, if not robotic performance. It demonstrated that he had a great deal of control of the feeling he did (or did not) put into the piece. Now he no longer felt helpless, and we were free to concentrate on the specific feelings he wished to convey, using methods such as guided fantasy.

This open approach is particularly useful in dealing with timing difficulties. Anxiety can easily disturb the rhythm of a- piece, even if the timing is well understood. Other times students just do not listen to what they play. Often timing goes awry before or after a group of quavers, usually because of a slight hesitation. Recently I had a student who was playing two quavers and a crotchet as dotted quaver, semiquaver, crotchet. The first quaver was too long, and the second too short. She knew there was a hiatus. Instead of directly correcting the timing, I asked her to see if she could measure the gap where she thought she was hesitating, just to see how long that space was in relation to those before and after. There is no right way to make such vague comparative measurements! She played the phrase again, this time absolutely accurately.

"Oh dear!" She said, "I can't measure it. I got it right! I'll try again."

She tried again, and got it right again. How frustrating!

Awareness of the hesitation banished it. This approach nearly always works. Ask for awareness, give permission to go
wrong, and the problem disappears. It is caused primarily by
lack of awareness compounded by anxiety.

I remember when I was first on the receiving end of this
approach, while working with Eloise Ristad. Eloise was a
wonderful teacher who led you gently to discover your
own powers, and the deeper processes that underlie any
musical activity.

I played a study involving a fast continuous right hand
arpeggio pattern. I was playing the pattern unevenly: my
fingers seemed to have a life of their own. Eloise surprised
me by asking me deliberately to do what I wanted to avoid. I
found I could not. When I tried to take control of the une-
venness, it vanished and I found the arpeggio was smooth! I
learned that these sorts of difficulties are actually caused by
all the effort that we make to overcome them.

Negative Practice

When students make a mistake, social upbringing whis-
pers "failure" and "try again, stupid" in their ear, and makes
them feel bad. This is a social tape-loop that needs to be
erased as soon as possible. To extend the metaphor, making
deliberate mistakes scrambles the recording. The tables are
turned. Now they must succeed at failing and know what it
is that they are trying to avoid. This technique has been
called "negative practice". Positive practice is clearly common sense, yet negative practice works too.

There is an unusual study by Reitmeyer (1972) on
the application of negative practice to the correction of
habitual fingering errors in clarinet performance. 25
clarinettists applied negative practice to half of their habitual
errors and positive practice to the other half. Negative
practice meant repeating the errors while being aware of
the correct fingering. Positive practice was simply playing
the correct fingering. At the end of the study, statistical
analysis showed that there was no significant difference
between the effectiveness or efficiency of the two opposing

methods in correcting the errors. The players' prior levels of musical achievement made no difference to their results either. This is a remarkable result and deserves to be more widely known. If negative practice was effective here, when presumably the subjects were not nervous about failing the test, then I think it is an extremely useful choice for a teacher, especially if the student is worried about "getting it right". It is also unusual and fun, two more reasons why it is likely to work.

Diversion

Diverting a student's attention is a powerful method of changing an unsatisfactory way of playing. Focusing on a mistake covertly reinforces it. (Don't think of the colour blue!). Diversion actually takes the attention to something else and breaks concentration. It is like becoming aware of how you tie your shoelaces and then trying to do it deliberately. Playing an instrument is a very complex activity. If I ask a student to do something incongruous, it will disrupt his strategic sequence and give him a fresh opportunity to see things in a new light, get a fresh grip, or sound out his playing anew. All playing has positive aspects of course, but if there are timing or technical difficulties then diversion tactics can work very well.

Unusual diversions are most effective. Asking a student to look at the clock in order to improve his rhythmic memory is certainly unusual. This is also an example of how interrupting accessing cues can lead to a change in response. Another example is asking a player to look downwards and not upwards when playing scales, to access kinaesthetically. Such things are also distractions from any anxious preoccupation with mistakes.

Kinaesthetic Diversions

Any student or performer who is anxious is liable to be very aware of his unpleasant internal feelings. Diverting the attention to other external feelings, especially breathing

will help. I often ask students to be aware of the tactile feel
of the guitar strings when they are playing. This is
something that has long passed into unconsciousness in
guitarists and making such a demand can make a student
radically review his playing and change his awareness. There
is no right way to feel a guitar string, so he cannot "fail"
either.

Visual Diversions

One visual distraction I use is to ask a student to play and
simply pay attention to how black the notes are on the page,
observing if some notes are blacker than others and to let
me know afterwards. This is so novel it frequently results
in a perfect performance. It is particularly effective with
sightreading. Students are often disappointed at not detecting any difference in blackness between the notes. (Should
there have been? Is that a wrong answer?) Asking for
awareness yields far more insight into playing than direct
suggestions or predetermined tests.

Auditory Diversions

Auditory diversions can be the most effective. If a student or group is having difficulty with a piece, I ask them to
listen to the tone. Listening is the very essence of music, yet
often the player is too busy making sure of the right notes,
right timing and good technique. All his available attention
are fully occupied. It is not good for any musician to be so
overloaded that there is no attention left over for listening.
Every musician hears his own playing, but does he listen to
it? Sometimes what he listens to is the internal version of
the piece. If he does this, he will miss mistakes because he is
hearing what he expects to hear, or more accurately, he will
not hear what he does not expect to hear. Listening is active,
hearing is passive. Listening improves the sound and gives
it a livelier quality immediately without trying. Listening to
the sound is also a very good way of distracting the busy
mind from thinking about the mistakes it must avoid (and

therefore is more likely to make).

I remember working with a student on the Bourrée from the first lute suite by J. S. Bach. Taryn was a creative and fluent guitarist. She did get rather nervous when playing to anyone else, and so did not always do herself justice.

This is the first section of the Bourrée:

I had told her before how the bass and treble voices could be played as two separate tunes. It is particularly important to bring out the bass voice. Our ears are too used to finding a tune in the treble, with the bass as an accompaniment, and this is not a good way to approach contrapuntal music. It is difficult to separate voices on the guitar, where the right hand thumb is the equivalent of the left hand on the piano, and the right hand fingers are the equivalent of the right hand on the piano. Independent control of thumb and fingers on the same hand is even more difficult than independent control of each hand on the piano.

Taryn thought she should be able to play the piece

and balance the voices, but found it very difficult. Her belief in what she "should" be able to do easily was getting in
the way of what she wanted to do. Finding she could not do
it, she thought she was at a dead end. She had a constant
internal voice that commented on and criticised her playing,
giving her an update on her mistakes.

I wanted to work on independent control of the bass and
treble, and also, clandestinely, to still this internal commentary. Firstly I sang the bottom voice, while she played the top
voice. Then I played the top voice while she sang the bottom voice. We sang and played the voices in various different combinations. Then we played it with the bass trans-
posed up an octave, and the treble down an octave, so it
sounded like this:

etc.

This certainly gave us a new perspective. When I asked
her to play it normally again, she found it much easier to
follow the parts. I asked her next to play the piece, this time
following neither part. This is very difficult, if not impossible. In fact it is much more difficult than following the
bass. I do not know and I cannot check what she did to follow this instruction. Taryn, perhaps because she was used
to strange musical instructions from me, played it again,
this time with clear voicing, and in a far more relaxed
way than before. Of course the singing and playing we did
had clarified the melodic flow of the voices, but more than
this, I felt that listening to neither voice prevented her
"trying" to play with the "right" balance, and so stopped
the self-critical internal commentary. I asked her to do
something at which she could not fail. Whenever she can
recapture that state of mind, she will play well, regardless of
what she thinks she should or should not be able to do.

Chapter Nine

Musical Standards

A standard is a nominalization that has a great deal of influence in education. Whose standards applied to whom, about what and by whom? The dictionary gives several meanings of the word, but there are three that seem to be applicable to music and education. The first definition is "The degree of excellence etc., required for a particular purpose..(as in does not come up to the standard)..." The second is "...measure to which others conform, or by which the accuracy of others is judged (standard pound) thus serving as a basis of comparison....." The third is simply "average quality as 'work was of a low standard'...".

All three involve a comparison or outside judgement applied to individuals and all have a lost performative. The first definition would refer to the realistic and pragmatic professional standards that students have to meet if they wish, for example, to be successful performers, or go to music college. These particular standards are formed by a consensus of performers, teachers and audiences in the world of music. The first definition would also refer to a music grade examination, where there is a fixed pass mark and standard of performance which you must attain on the day. You will pass or fail purely on your own merits.

The second definition could reasonably apply to a definite measure, such as a pound or a metre, but comparing people is quite different. A meaningful comparison of achievement levels is impossible unless the levels are narrowly specified. Applying the Meta Model to such a standard soon reveals its limitations. Everyone is unique. Like can only be compared with like. This definition does not specify the comparison by which the standard is judged, or how it is to be measured.

Standards give rise to expectations, teachers will expect certain skills of their students over a particular time scale and students will have their own expectations of progress. The expectations of teachers, parents and students may not be realistic, they may be unrelated to the student's individual talents, strengths and weaknesses.

Self-fulfilling Prophecies

First of all, teachers may pitch their expectations too low. Young students will tend to be influenced and form a self-image based on what adults expect of them. The external expectations become internalized as a belief; they mould responses more subtly than do direct admonitions. Low expectations then become self-fulfilling prophecies and can drastically affect performance in the long and short terms. Many people have beliefs that limit what they can do. There is a saying, whether you think you can or cannot do something, *you're right*.

To give a simple example from my own teaching. One of my students was warming up in a lesson by playing scales to a metronome. She had started slowly and I was increasing the speed one notch at a time. We eventually reached a speed that caused her to falter.

After several unsuccessful attempts she told me:

"That's too fast, my fingers can't move that quickly yet."

I said I would go back a notch to her maximum speed so she could carry on playing. In fact I did nothing of the sort, I left the speed unchanged. She then did the scale perfectly.

This was not supposed to be a speed test, and we were not interested in the actual speed in beats per minute. It was just a warming-up exercise. I told her I had tricked her to find out how far the limit was self-imposed. Jill expected to fail at the 'high' speed and did. She succeeded at the 'lower' speed because she already knew she could do it. I am afraid this trick will not work indefinitely, but it does show clearly how performance is influenced by expectations.

Any belief predisposes you to notice facts that support it, and ignore facts that dispute it. Studies have been done with children divided into two groups of approximately equal aptitude. Teachers were told that one group had a high IQ and were expected to do better than the second group. This became a self-fulfilling prophecy. (The Pygmalion effect).

Teachers noticed the achievements of the 'bright' children and the failures of the 'dumb' ones. This categorising had nothing to do with the children themselves or their possible learning powers (Rosenthal and Jacobsen).

The 'bright' children picked up the signal that they were expected to do well and were motivated to build on their successes and not to be worried about their failures. The opposite was true for the other group. Teachers need to be careful that a negative attitude towards students does not become a self-fulfilling prophecy.

An interesting experiment was carried out at Keele University, showing dramatically how expectations can alter perceptions in music. 40 undergraduate students took part in an experiment to see how their reaction to a piece of music was affected by the composer's reputation. 20 were told the truth, which was that the music was by a critically acclaimed composer of international standing. The other 20 were told the piece was by a fictitious semi-professional composer of considerably lower reputation. None of the students had heard the piece before, or had any reason to be suspicious. They were asked to rate the music on a scale of interest, emotional effect, and willingness to hear more works by the same composer.

The result was that those who thought the piece was by an established composer rated the music higher in every way than those who believed the composer was unacclaimed. It made no difference whether the undergraduates involved were music students or not.

Teachers' expectations have a placebo effect. A placebo is a neutral chemical given by doctors to patients who are expecting a helpful medicine. Placebos are used in clinical trials to check that any improvement is actually due to the administered drug and not the patient's expectations. However, body and mind interact so much that it is impossible to distinguish the physical effects of the drug from those caused primarily by the patient's mental state. It has been shown many times that patients given placebos can improve as much as patients given the actual medicine. The improvement depends on a belief in the doctor's skill and the medicine he prescribes, just as the student's belief in his teacher or in his own ability, leads him to do better in his studies. Success breeds success. Perhaps all sorts of technical exercises given to students are placebos. You cannot necessarily attribute the patient's recovery to the direct effect of the medicine, nor a student's progress to the exercises. The personality of the teacher is a more potent factor and the inner resources of the student are the most important of all. In practical terms teachers who look for the best from their students and believe in their talents will help bring out the very talents they are looking for.

Ideal Standards

Unrealistically high standards are just as damaging, though in a different way, as low standards. They do not act as self-fulfilling prophecies because they are unreachable by definition. They are usually based on what people think "should" happen as opposed to the real world. There is great pressure on everyone for results. Young people may have unrealistic demands made on them, and their expectations of what they can do may be set too high. The two things tend to go together, it sometimes seems that nothing short of perfection is acceptable. Children are liable to grow up with the conviction that nothing they do will ever be good enough if teachers and parents constantly set impossibly high standards, and make constant criticism of their efforts to do what they can in the here and now.

So often teachers feel compelled to pass critical comment. Lessons need not be places where students go to find out how bad they are. What is a reasonable demand on one child may be impossible for another. One certain way of making someone feel inadequate is to ask for some arbitrary high standard, unrelated to his development, then do not give him permission to fail.

If expectations are set unrealistically high, students may expect to play a piece straight away and get instant results. There may also be constant time pressure, so they cannot wait for real and worthwhile results - these seem to come too slowly. Instrumentalists may believe they must practise for hours on end to improve their playing. The more painful this is and the more they force themselves to do it, the better they think they will become. It must be a six hour practice session or nothing. This sort of 'will power' which is so greatly prized in some educational circles is actually an egoistical thuggery practised by one part of the personality on another. The results are not wholehearted and therefore not very successful. Mastering any skill takes time and effort, but not the effort of trying to pull yourself into the air by your own bootstraps. The two opposing forces are part of the same system so the effort gets nowhere, all it does is provide unnecessary and self-defeating hard work. It is rather like a cat chasing its own tail. A cat does not try harder to catch its tail either, except in fun. It is revealing that sometimes the actual playing done is devalued if it falls short of vaulting ambition. 'Only' three hours practice! Not good enough! Unrealistic goals attract unrealistic means of achieving them.

Since perfection is impossible, and what is expected may be unreasonable, students will become discouraged and give up, thereby reinforcing the idea that they are not good enough. I believe everyone deserves an opportunity to develop their own musical abilities at their own pace, so a time limit that is not related to their personal development must not be applied. Musical maturity, like physical maturity, is an organic growth of the whole person. To force matters is in no-one's best interest. It is ironic that with arbitrary limits, and poor learning methods, skills will not be securely developed before they are guillotined by the time limit. Knowledge can be gained much more quickly if natural, unforced methods are used. Limits themselves can make students anxious that time will run out, and anxiety compounds the initial difficulty.

A lesson needs to be a time set aside when teacher and student can discover together what to do and generate an enthusiasm that carries them both along. Instrumental lessons, or any lessons, will create their own momentum. This cannot be forced. Everything that happens is grist to the mill including (or especially) the mistakes. The whole process is quite fascinating and no outside judgements or comparisons are admitted because these have nothing to do with the process as it unfolds.

The idea of an unfolding process is opposed to the usual way we deal with our achievements. One day you may be a learner driver, only allowed to drive in the company of a qualified driver. The next day, if you pass your test, you may be a qualified driver, able in turn to accompany learners. You have not changed, it is just that society has suddenly licensed you.

This is a useful and pragmatic way to arrange some things, but the trap is to assume that some sort of magical transformation has, or should have, taken place just because we have passed an examination or reached a certain age. Society marks out particular times for people to assume particular responsibilities, but this is not the way knowledge is actually gained.

Always looking forward to a time when you can, or will be able to do something, neglects the present moment and your actual, real skills. This is the only time you have to gain the expertise you want. Working with an eye on the future ensures always feeling uncertain in the present because you are distracted from learning what is needed when it is available.

I have been asked many times "How long was it before you could play the guitar sir?" This question shows the state of mind encouraged by ideal standards. It is difficult to think of learning as a gradual process when society licenses progress in quantum leaps. There is no time when you can sit back and say "Now I can play the guitar." Aiming for a magic time when you can 'play the guitar' is a distraction from real though gradual attainments in the present.

Children often ask me when they will be able to play the guitar and I am sure every instrumental teacher is asked this sort of question about his chosen instrument. The truthful answer must be "You can already!" There is also the implied question "When will I reach perfection and not have to learn any more?" I try to answer this question too, by explaining that such a state does not exist; if it did, it would be boredom incarnate.

There is no absolute time or state when you can play the

guitar (or do anything else), as opposed to being unable to do so. There is only continuous progress. Your view of what can be done, and what you want to do changes with time. Learning music is an exciting lifetime journey.

Another similar question is "How should this piece sound?" Again the implication here is a once and for all interpretation of the piece - a right answer that will satisfy an outside standard. The answer is that I do not know how the student is going to make it sound. I can offer guidelines, but interpretations grow and change with time, any final answer puts a stop to learning. If we judge our work on the basis of some ideal interpretation or standard of performance, then all we are left with is a continuous effort to attain a state that recedes further whenever we seem to approach it and a measure of our own inadequacy compared with the ideal, which by definition can never be reached. This is an unhappy state of affairs, but a very common one.

Everybody learns at his or her own pace. This individual style is the only standard applicable to that person. Ideal standards, like ideal musical interpretations are imaginary; they have nothing to do with the here and now. The present moment is the only place to start.

Ideals encourage a back-to-front view of education which starts from a perfect finished product and not from actual learners. Teaching is then tailored to produce this, as if learners are teachers with bits missing. Music students are not mature players with bits missing. It is impossible to pinpoint any stage where enough has been added for the learner to feel secure. In fact, taking this view, a student will always feel insecure because he is always searching for completion and this is impossible to obtain, by the very rules of the game.

In Greek mythology, Sisyphus was condemned to roll a stone up a hill forever because it would always tumble down just as he reached the summit. Having ideal standards is rather like the labours of Sisyphus. Once the realisation comes that there are no teachers, only learners using the same process to learn different things, then the damaging comparisons, and the hunt for the Chimera of completion can be dropped with a sigh of relief.

Skills can seem like all-or-nothing possessions. So many children say to me "I can't read music" just after they have played a piece on the guitar from the printed music. I say "But you just did!" and they reply "Oh yes, I can play that, but I can't read music really." They see reading music as the ultimate pinnacle of achievement, rather than something they do all the time, with growing competence.

Testing

Bearing in mind that learning is a shared process, and the student and teacher make contributions that are filtered linguistically and through both personalities, testing has nothing to do with learning. Testing is asking a question to elicit an answer you have already decided on. All a teacher ever has to work with are a student's perceptions at any particular time and testing does not relate to these, it relates only to the perceptions and preoccupations of the teacher. I am glad instrumental playing usually resists this empty kind of testing. Testing generates anxiety and nobody likes being tested. Children usually stop to guess or intuit which answer the teacher wants, of the many that may be available. If they cannot do this they say they do not know: they do not know which answer you want. They may actually know the piece of knowledge. It might seem so obvious to them that they are sure there is a catch somewhere, or the answer would not be so simple.

It is very interesting to give up testing, in other words not to ask any question you know the answer to already. I stopped asking questions like "What is a time signature?" or even "Do you know what a time signature is?" The latter question only asks for a yes or no reply, but is my representation of a time signature the same as the student's? I try to bear in mind that the answer I would give to even such a straightforward question as this has changed over time. The student's hesitation over such a question is often due to the fact that the actual question she is asking herself is "Do I know what *he* means by a time signature?" Testing children by asking questions to find out what they know is not very effective. Firstly they will not understand the question in the same way you do, because they do not have your knowledge and therefore you will not understand their answer, if they make one, in the way they mean it.

I remember asking a group of eight-year olds what they thought the treble clef signified. The most popular answer was that it started the music. This is true, but it was not the answer I had in mind. The one I most liked was from a small boy who said he thought the treble clef was there to make the music sound beautiful. This made my answer sound somewhat prosaic.

This sort of communication problem is more acute with children, for they learn in a less conscious fashion than adults. Their experience is limited and their knowledge and use of language is less sophisticated. Adults have a much greater series of skills and a body of knowledge that is tried and tested. They know it and have confidence in it and know that they know. They can also express it in words, for their left brain linguistic capacities are well developed.

A child may know the answer to a question, but not know they know it. They may be able to accomplish a musical task, but imagine they cannot. When they try and succeed, this knowledge becomes conscious and available. A teacher's work is to allow this to unfold in its own time.

Students become so used to testing that they often view straightforward requests for information as tests. When I try to find out how much a student knows about music and the guitar when he first starts lessons with me, I often get the impression that he feels it is highly dangerous to admit to knowing anything. Firstly, because he may be wrong. Secondly, I may not agree with him; thirdly, he may be tested further and fourthly, he may feel just plain uncertain about knowledge which has not been validated at all levels by the voice of authority.

Grade Examinations

Instrumental   music   examinations   are   a   slightly
different proposition to testing. No-one is forced to take
them, but   they can become an end in themselves.   To
exchange the joy of making music for its own sake for working to get   the   next   grade   is a poor bargain. Music
examinations   should   be   as   rational   and   inwardly
consistent as possible, but even this is not always true. Like
all   examinations, they are   also   arbitrary standards; not
sacrosanct, autonomous measures fixed for all time.

In order to achieve grade three you have to demonstrate
certain skills to an examiner. These skills comprise grade
three, and grade three is these skills because someone has
decided so in the past. Tomorrow it could be different.
Looked at in this way, grade examinations need not be
disturbing. They are only worth doing as a challenge to
yourself and do not magically make you a better player.

Of course examinations also take place at a single, unique
time. If you fail, it means only that you did not meet the
standard on that particular occasion. Yet on the basis of
these particular occasions musical futures may be judged.
Examinations are stressful by their very nature, even though
the examiners are nearly always friendly.

I   enter students for grade examinations only at their
own suggestion, and I try to make as certain as humanly
possible that they pass. In fact there is no need for any candidate to fail on the technical or musical content of a grade
examination. If a student wants to enter, and is not doing the
grade for someone else's vicarious satisfaction, he is under
no pressure to take it until he is ready. If he does fail, then
this is a statement about his 'examination nerves', or the
congruence (or lack of it) between the examiner's and the
teacher's view of a pass standard at that level. Luckily,
there are seldom any very important consequences of
success or failure in a grade examination.

Conscious and conscientious preparation of the skill and
musicianship needed is the important thing, and if this
has been done, then the result is secondary. It is a trick

really, because at the climactic point (ie. the actual test), all the important work is over. Pass or fail, this can never be taken away.

There is social importance attached to tangible results however, so that failure makes it seem as if all the work was for nothing. Instead, it means only that the candidate did not meet the standard on that day.

So examinations are useful as an outside challenge and stimulus for skill and achievement. Grade examinations have a criteria-referenced pass. This means that the candidate will pass or fail purely on his performance at that time, regardless of the standard of other candidates. This is a much more natural system than a norm-referenced pass. There, the passmark is fixed on the basis of failing a certain percentage of entrants, so regardless of how well you do, you may still fail if enough people do better than you. It means it is possible to pass the examination with a lower mark than someone who failed the year before. This is not a test of skill, but a competitive comparison.

Comparison and Competition

Competitions which are based on comparative judgements of people are only useful if they are used as an opportunity to combat and go beyond nervousness and self-restraints. Any opponent is really your friend, he is there to give you an opportunity to express your skill freely and fulfil your talent.

The competitive view of the world is built on the fallacy that success involves being better than other people, and so your own sense of worth comes from a comparison with others and is dependent on others, rather than being based on your own resources and existence as a person in your own right. No-one has to be measured by anybody else. If your only opponent is your own limitations, then nobody has to lose. No-one can truly be judged from a limited and comparative point of view. Stopping competitions in the interests of spurious egalitarianism, so that the losers do not feel bad and worthless is not the answer. This response is still caught up in the belief that a person's worth is actually measured by competition and comparison with others. People are demonstrably not equal in certain respects, and it is damaging and deluding to pretend that they are. It does not mean however that they are in any way inferior, of less value, or do not have the resources to change. Self-esteem does not depend on comparison. 'Losers' have nothing to feel bad about.

Judging yourself by comparison with others and striving to be a winner in these terms, in fact turns you into a loser. As it is impossible to win all the time, there will be many times when you lose, and therefore feel bad. For me, music is about sharing with others, not competing with them.

Judgements give snapshots of people at particular points in time, they cannot take into account all the myriad things that precede and follow this photographic instant. Clinging to the snapshot will miss the contemporary picture. Examinations are examples of such a polaroid way of looking at things.

Comparisons create a barrier. Praise and blame are what follow. Praise and compliments based on comparisons may seem worthwhile but they are really useless. Praise by comparison with others is an implicit criticism, for it is not direct praise for the person, their worth and the worth of their work, but simply placement in a hierarchy. A student may be stimulated to work by competitive comparison with siblings, classmates or other students. This can be a powerful motivation, but not a constructive one. It will not last. It is actually antagonistic to the student's long term interests and happiness. A student who is treated as a unique individual with great possibilities will be encouraged to give his best, regardless of what his neighbour might be doing.

Chapter Ten

Social Attitudes

To return to our starting point; learning and teaching are communication: a two-way process. The meaning of a communication is the response it gets, and on this criterion, a lot of education is useless, even damaging, it provokes the opposite to its intention. It makes no sense for teachers to say they taught children a subject, which the children perversely did not learn. There is also a group of ideas that oppose teacher to learner, as if the two are engaged in some sort of battle, instead of a shared task.

We all have ideas concerning how to learn, built up mostly from how we were taught. There are implicit assumptions in any educational system that encourage a particular model of teaching and learning, and these will determine how we see ourselves, and treat others, as learners. Most of the ideas about learning come from our experience of school, where social values are transmitted, and learning and teaching become formalised by the structure of the education system. Many outside factors such as type of premises and numbers of children influence the way the system is organised. These in turn restrict the way that subjects are taught. The outside model, or organization, tends to mould how we think of the inside process, but one need not reflect the other.

General assumptions about education must be questioned, for they limit the possible range of responses for teacher and learner. If teaching methods and what is expected of students are narrowly defined, students will tend to accept these limits as part of their education. They become self-imposed. Students then respond by making less use of their abilities, thus backing up the initial model. The cycle is self-perpetuating.

The way in which subjects are taught and the way in which learners are treated gives a powerful underlying message quite apart from the subject matter concerned. This message is stronger than any other because it is constant. Lesson subjects change, whereas the way they are taught stays the same.

There is too much emphasis on teaching, and not enough on learning. Teaching is seen as a skilful occupation, even a mysterious and difficult activity, and learning is linked with passivity, difficulty and dullness. The teacher is assumed to be the active one, but really learning is the active process and happens often despite teaching, not because of it.

A student's resistance or difficulty (and this includes "learning disabilities") is only feedback on a teacher's method. This is not failure for teacher or student, but a very valuable piece of information: this particular student does not respond to this approach, so it it time to try something else.

As education is generally assumed to be about teaching, both teachers and students can be lulled into the feeling that if a subject is covered, then it is (or should be) learnt. Many, many times I have asked a question such as "What is a treble clef?" and received an answer like "Oh yes, we did that last week in class." Then there is an expectant silence. This is no answer at all. The implication is that if something is done in class, then it is known in some mysterious way that absolves everyone of further reponsibility. This is the Vaccination Theory of education, it states that if you have done a subject, you do not need to do it again, you are immune. The theory is present in epidemic proportions in schools.

Facts come up repeatedly from a multitude of angles, each time with richer associations and meanings. The Vaccination Theory is based on the fallacy that teaching equals learning, and if something has been taught, then it is automatically learned.

There is also a great deal of evidence to show that children can learn even more quickly from their peers who are more in rapport with them and so more able to help. If I am working with an ensemble, and someone is having difficulty, I always ask one of the more experienced players to help him. It saves time and is usually more effective than doing it myself.

Individual Attitudes

Students, (and teachers), bring all sorts of ideas and preconceptions to any teaching situation, especially if it is one to one. They have a chance to confront them there, or negative ideas may be strong enough to sabotage any long-term learning. In a few cases lessons may become annoying instead of pleasant: if the ideas are out of awareness they cannot be countered by any reasonable arguments. These sorts of ideas are the mental equivalents of physical habits. They are what take over when we do not know what we are doing. Unless we are aware of them, we are not in a position to choose whether we want to keep them or not. Sometimes superficially obvious questions hide much deeper issues.

I remember a particular lesson with a girl named Carol. We were going over a section of music which involved the repeated use of the left hand fourth finger to stop a string. Of course this is the weakest finger and the one students will try to avoid using as much as humanly possible, despite the fact that use cures weakness, so it really could be the one to use the most. Because she was not using the fourth finger, the music was staccato, and I pointed this out.

"But I can do it this way." she said, going into incredible digital contortions, that looked twice as difficult as the fingering she was trying to avoid.

"Only just," I said. "Surely it is easier to use the fourth finger?"

"But why? I don't need to."

"Why limit yourself to three-quarters of your playing strength by leaving out the fourth finger?"

"But I can't do it your way."

"What stops you?"

"..........Anyway, I might give up the guitar next term, or you might leave the school, so it probably won't make any difference in the long run." she said with a seraphic smile.

This was when I felt a flash of annoyance. I felt like telling her not to be ridiculous, to play the finger I said because I said it was best and be quiet. I sensed we were not talking about left hand fingering at all.

"If you run your life that way, there's no point in doing anything. I might die tomorrow but that is not going to alter what is best to do now, all the more reason to do it."

"Have you tried my fingering?" she asked.

"No."

"How do you know my way of playing isn't best for me then? My friend never uses her little finger. Her teacher says you don't need it and he plays really well."

"I don't think you really believe in your method. You only want to find out the justification for mine."

"Why should I always have to do things your way ?"

These sorts of arguments are difficult to answer, and I cast round for a reply that did not pull rank, or say in effect I know better than you, do it my way. A good reply would have been "What would be a valid reason for you to want to do it this way?" I did not think of this at the time. The point is, it is not my way, but a way based on the way hands work and the pooled experience of many guitarists. I hoped she would see it was logically better. I had no way of forcing her to do it.

In effect she was questioning the basis of my authority. Ultimately perhaps it is only a wider viewpoint based on my own experience, and my knowledge of the experience of others.

At the end of the lesson she turned round and said casually "Well, I'll probably try it your way."

I believe everyone will strive to use his or her talents to the greatest possible degree. Situations and attitudes can block a student's musical progress, even though everything looks good on the surface. Regular attendance at lessons is no guarantee that anything is going to change. There are more dimensions to a lesson than the simple learning of musical skills. There is the social dimension, or what generally held ideas and attitudes influence the lesson. There is also the emotional dimension: how the feelings of the teacher and student interact. The lesson does not take place in a vacuum, and the connection needs to be explored.

Seldom if ever, are we single-minded about anything.

It is a matter of degree. Students come to lessons for a variety of reasons. If the balance is good, and it nearly always is, we can work. If not, there will be difficulties. I hope to be able to work so my students can become more skilful guitarists and better musicians, and we can learn from each other. They have permission to do as well as they want to. I will not be caught in a game where the less they do, the more I worry. I am responsible only for my own musical progress. I am not responsible for the musical progress of anyone else. This is very important. It saves me from many sleepless nights, and lessons have a more relaxed atmosphere where discoveries can be made. It relieves both myself and my students of a worrisome burden.

Lessons do not always go smoothly, and sometimes when it becomes obvious that we have come to a standstill, which does not happen very often, it is for me to question why and to say what I think is happening as constructively as possible. This is the only way forward. It can be very difficult to judge exactly when things have gone far enough to speak out, but these questions of attitude are just as relevant as technical ones, and unless they are solved, technical and musical points cannot be dealt with.

Sue had passed grade five when she first came to me for lessons in school at the beginning of term, saying she wanted to study for grade six. She already had the music, so we agreed to work together towards the examination. She forgot to come to three of the first ten lessons, and arrived late for five more. She forgot her music on nearly every occasion. As half term holidays had come and gone, it meant we had done very little in three months. She had done some desultory practice. The tenth week she brought her music, and asked me if she could leave it in the music room at the end of the lesson, and collect it that evening as she did not want to have to carry it round the school. I said she could, and I would leave it on the table in the middle of the room when I went home. The next week she came and asked me for her music (which she had only missed that morning).

I thought I had better put my cards on the table to join

her music. I told her that what she did contradicted what
she said she wanted to do. She kept saying she wanted to
take grade six, but absolutely nothing was happening. I said
if she was here on time and I came late most weeks, sometimes forgot to come, and did not bring any of the music
we were to study, she would soon begin to wonder if I really
wanted to teach her at all. She had expected me to keep her
book and give it to her that week, despite what I had said
about leaving it on the table, which she seemed to have con-
veniently forgotten.   Without the book of course she could
not play the music at home.

Her actions suggested two unspoken attitudes to me.
Firstly I was being tested on my memory for the music, and
secondly by forgetting what I had said, she tried to put me
in a position where I was responsible for her not practising,
because I had kept her book. It might be better to say that she
had tried to give me the responsibility for her progress
right from the start. If I play this game, Sue will blame me
for her lack of progress and probable eventual failure at
grade six (if I am fool enough to enter her). As I had not co-
operated, this was a last desperate attempt to see if I would
assume responsibility.

I was very slow to see what she was trying to tell me, but
blaming or accusing her would have missed the point en-
tirely. I explained what I thought was happening, and after
this we understood each other better. I agreed to give her
very clear instructions on exactly what to do and she agreed
to find time to do it.

Sue is the sort of person who needs clear instructions
and a definite structure to be able to work. Sometimes students just will not play whatever teaching they are given.
This is because the balance has shifted, and they are no
longer coming to lessons primarily to learn the guitar.
They may like and admire the teacher, and this is good,
but if the relationship becomes unbalanced so that the student is coming mainly to be with the teacher and not
to learn, it creates a difficult situation. Students may attend
regularly for weeks, but hardly play from one lesson to the
next. This will only show itself over some period of time,
and is difficult to   deal with. The students themselves may

not be fully aware of why they come, or what is happening, but the teacher needs to be. Perhaps all that can be done is to point out the discrepancy between what they say they want, and what they are actually doing. They say they wish to learn, but are not fulfilling their part of the bargain. You can ask them what they are going to do about it.

It is not surprising that students will seek out the company of a man or women who seems powerful and successful in what he or she does, for this is what they wish too.

Responsibility

The most valuable teaching gives a student more knowledge, more freedom, and more choices than he had before. Giving the student responsibility for his own learning is an important part of this approach. The process of learning any skill is comparable, in a small way, to the process of growing up. The student is guided constantly to a point where he can make his own decisions. Different students will take up responsibility at different rates, and at different stages. It is not an all-or-nothing situation. The teacher holds the responsibility in trust, it is always on offer for when the student decides he wants it.

The educational system takes the opposite view, and children are given little educational responsibility to control their own learning; often their active responsibility begins and ends with getting to the right place at the right time. The rest is a matter of sitting still, paying attention and trusting to the Vaccination Theory.

Instead, students need every opportunity to do things for themselves in all sorts of different ways to see the results. Arguably, the student's presence at the lesson implies that he wants help from the teacher, but exactly what sort of help? Thinking in terms of a one-way passage of 'help', makes the student the weaker party and the teacher the powerful one, and fixes the situation that way. A better approach is to see two people, one more experienced than the other, exploring the process of learning a musical skill. If there is any question of experts, then it is the student who is the expert in his own skills, insights, capabilities and weaknesses. Sometimes students will certainly want the teacher's contribution, other times they will not, and it will only complicate matters if the teacher interferes.

Unasked for help has been likened to theft. It is taking away another person's opportunity to learn something through his own efforts, and by exercising his own power. It is much better to notice and correct your own mistakes whenever possible than to have someone do it for you. Students will do this more and more as they find out that you are not, and do not claim to be a magician, and do not take responsibility or credit for their successes or failures. They are much more likely to remember something they discover for themselves than something they are told.

If learners, (especially young children), are defined as helpless and irresponsible and then define themselves as such, a crushing burden falls on the back of the teacher, who is then seen as having all the power and responsibility. This is a totally unnecessary and self-inflicted burden and it causes a great deal of stress and hardship to conscientious teachers. The kind of help that prevents a person from doing things he needs to do for himself, or does things for him that he can do already, is useless. The more this sort of help is given, the more helpless he becomes, and the more frustrating it is for all parties.

Everyone resents being made helpless and will make life difficult for those who treat them as if they are. The only way they can exercise any influence on events is to block them. Hence the frustration for both sides. It becomes a game and I am sure that when children perceive these facts clearly they can be very good players. There are advantages to be had by appearing helpless. Of course, it is self-defeating in the long run.

Students who are not allowed to take some responsibility for their own learning, regardless of age, are likely to learn to be stupid, so that teachers can teach them. They will learn that learning is hard, that knowledge is specialised and that it is transmitted only through special people. They will learn that passive acceptance is valued, and short-term recall of facts is very highly valued. They will learn that there is an answer to every question and what is more, there is a right answer to every question (and many wrong ones). It is assumed that children are ignorant and cannot learn without help. Ignorance equals stupidity. In order to prosper in such a system, children must pretend to be as ignorant and stupid as possible.

The Teacher as a Magician

If students believe themselves to be helpless, they may well feel they have nothing to contribute. They can passively rely on the teacher to transfer his knowledge magically. It is important to let students have positive responsibility and power over their own learning, otherwise you will be cast in the role of a magician, which is very tiring and exasperating. Children are treated as helpless and irresponsible as learners, yet are blamed and held responsible if they do not learn despite being taught. You cannot make people responsible in one breath, and treat them as irresponsible in the next; you put them in a double bind where whatever they do is wrong.

Defining children as ignorant and incompetent adults who cannot help themselves, puts a heavy burden on the teacher and means that education itself becomes the panacea to answer this problem. To remedy all the imposed helplessness and ignorance more education is called for. It occupies the position therefore of being both poison and antidote. It is a iatrogenic disease, one that is caused and sustained, by the supposed cure. The answer is not more of this sort of education, but less.

There is another danger in putting so much emphasis on the teacher's knowledge and skill, without paying attention to the student's powers of learning. Some students think that mere attendance at instrumental lessons will somehow magically enable them to improve by some sort of osmosis. Many of the assumptions in the educational system encourage them to think this way. Much time is wasted while the Osmosis Theory is disproved.

When learning is considered as a process, students and teachers are equal. Both wish to increase their knowledge. A student will be trying to solve a technical and musical problem using the resources at his disposal, (and these include the teacher). I will be doing exactly the same in my own playing. My technical and musical problems may be different from his, but the process we use to solve them is the same. We are therefore equal.

The teacher/learner situation is usually defined in an unbalanced way. It is not normally treated as a partnership of equals discovering knowledge together, one more experienced than the other. It is defined instead in terms of strong and weak. To be a learner in the presence of a teacher is a rather daunting prospect, especially if the learner is a child. This does not mean that teachers necessarily try to make it this way, (although some do), but this is how the students themselves tend to see it and so, for them, this is how it actually is. The teacher can take on an almost magical aura of skill. The less you play the guitar to your students, the better player you will be thought to be: do not touch the guitar throughout the lesson if you wish to appear a maestro. Most impressive of all is to play the piano instead.

I remember an incident in a group class that will illustrate some of these points. The class was working on an ensemble quartet, and talking about their tendency to speed up while playing. We started discussing ways to demonstrate this, and I foolishly began boasting of my ability to get exactly £10 worth of petrol from an automatic pump by gauging its speed of delivery for the first gallon and then closing my eyes while still counting. I would stop the pump when my internal count reached £10, and I was usually exactly right.

Ray then challenged me to measure out a minute by his watch if he counted me in. I immediately felt unsure and rather anxious. Most of the others had tried it and had been about 5 to 10 seconds out. When I did it, I was also a few seconds out and not much better than anybody else. Then a strange thing happened. Everybody started to make excuses for me. It was acceptable for them to be inaccurate, but not

for me. I learned a great deal that night. I learned how students must feel when tested and how they tend to keep
teachers as superior beings. I also saw my own tendency to
set myself up as better than everyone else. The class
mythology still remembers me as being much better than
anyone else in the stopwatch test.

Enforced Practice

The strongest motivation comes from the student
himself. Given responsibility, he can take charge of his
own musical journey. I will help him as much as I can. If
all goes well, he will want to practise. Enforced practice is liable to create resentment and resistance because enforce-
ment implies his own reources are not enough.

One aspect of enforced practice is the keeping of practice
reports for children. I think these are a destructive waste
of time. A practice report normally consists of a form for
the parent to sign, signifying that the child has done the
required daily practice time laid down by the teacher. It operates on the assumption that time spent is an absolute
measure of progress made and half an hour spent at the
guitar is better than half an hour spent elsewhere. One
reaction to being forced to do something you do not want
to do is to while away the time until allowed to do something else. The practice report may show regular times
spent, but the student's playing may be no better for it.
This can lead to trouble, the guitar becoming an unpleasant
duty and the joy of music-making being lost. Parents also
resent this chore and the battle it can cause.

Practice reports also imply that unless some sort of check
is being kept, no playing would be done and that the student is untrustworthy. Only by giving someone the chance
to be unreliable can they prove themselves trustworthy. If
you treat people as being unworthy of trust, they will
often become so. It may become a self-fulfilling prophecy
and create what it is trying to avoid. The student is the
loser if he does not play; he presumably wishes to improve,
otherwise he would not be coming to lessons. If parents
are paying for lessons then they can stop them at any time

if they wish.

These reports are unlikely to lead to the wished-for improvement (wished for by whom?). Unless a student feels he owns his playing, he is unlikely to put himself wholeheartedly into it.

Sometimes I forbid students to practise. I remember a student who was under a good deal of pressure in her work at both home and school. She was studying for grade three on both the piano and recorder as well as playing the guitar. She owned a very good guitar which deserved to be played. She started to feel under an obligation to play. She was made to practise every night, and our lessons deteriorated. She said she wanted to study for a grade, so we started to do some work on these lines but it soon became clear that this was not what she really wanted. She could not openly frustrate me or her parents by refusing to practise, but she could make sure that however much 'practice' she did, she never got any better. Her own motivation had been lost in the demands of others.

I felt the best way to use the lesson was to play duets in an atmosphere that was as relaxed and easy as possible. I seldom corrected her. She knew if she made a mistake. She resented her enforced nightly practice, and was starting to resent music. I forbade her to practise and told her parents so. She thought this was a wonderful idea. There were several weeks when she played very little.

Now the tables were turned, for when she played outside the lesson, it was in defiance of orders, and so much more enjoyable - when she did not, she was obeying me. It is rather like Judo, using your opponent's momentum to defeat him. Not that I regarded her as an opponent to defeat. I was not concerned whether she played or not. I made her take responsibility for her own playing.

Lessons started to be fun again. Slowly she regained her interest and ability. I reluctantly allowed her, in a rather theatrical way, to play the guitar only when she felt like it. Consequently the times she felt like playing became more frequent. She enjoys playing the guitar now, whereas before she was considering giving up.

The drudgery of enforced practice can take all the joy from music. Fritz Kreisler, the renowned violinist, was reported as saying "I never practise: it takes the bloom from my playing". A student may not actually want to give up the instrument, but has to, in order to give up the practice schedule; the two get inextricably associated. I know a girl who "accidentally" left her clarinet on the bus to avoid practising. She had been made to practise and wanted to stop. Her name and address were inside the case, so it was returned after a few days. She did not really want to lose it permanently, but she did not want to play it either. The more she had to play, the less she enjoyed it. I think it is very sad if anyone actually comes to hate music because they are made to do it, yet this does happen to many people.

I remember talking with a friend some time ago about my difficulty in getting through to a student. I described the means I was employing to get her to play. None were successful, and I thought she would probably give up. I said it would be a pity if she did; she had talent and ought to use it. My friend pointed out that I was making a value judgement. I was indignant. It seemed obvious to me that playing was better than giving up: it is a wonderful thing to make music. But I had still made an unsupported value judgement that it was better for her at that particular time in her life. It took me some time to see his point of view, but now I am sure it is right. Whatever worthwhile things we do, we cannot decide what is best for other people. Only they can do this. What is more we must let them be free to do so.

Motivation

The most important factor is the student's motivation. He must want to learn. A student will be motivated to learn an instrument if he sees it as relevant, interesting and enjoyable. As time goes by his enthusiasm may vary, it will be at its highest in the first few lessons.

As long as he enjoys what he is doing he will continue. I do not believe this enjoyment or interest can be forced.

The worst reason of all for learning something is because somebody is making you.

Every student will have his own reasons for learning. His friends may be learning and he does not want to be left out. He may think of it as a stepping stone to playing lead guitar in a rock band. The usefulness of everything I say and demonstrate will be judged from a completely different standpoint. Often the lessons themselves will change a student's viewpoint, I have had many who initially wished to do chords, but became caught up in reading music and stopped folk playing, discovering with delight the guitar's classical repertoire instead.

We learn things easily when we need to know them. This is when enthusiasm is at its height. Many things I feel I "ought" to do are not actually relevant at the time and serve only to make me feel guilty. When I need to know them, I can learn them easily.

I can remember many students who made great progress both musically and technically when they wanted to learn pieces that I thought were too difficult for them. They had to improve, or they could not play their chosen piece.

Sometimes I like to bring out the power of motivation in a particularly graphic way. One student complained that she could not do a piece because her left hand fourth finger was too weak. She implied there was nothing she could do about it. I wanted to convince her that this actually meant she did not want to change it.

I said "Suppose there was an absolute way of measuring the strength of your fourth finger by a sort of 'test your strength machine'. This machine will give an exact reading of the strength in your little finger. Now suppose I said I would give you £100 if you could double your reading on this machine by next week's lesson. What would you do?"

The answer to this question is the answer to the original problem. Of course I did say this was definitely an imaginary situation, I do not bribe students in quite such tangible ways. I was just trying to make the point clearly that given sufficient reason to do something, we can usually find the time and resources to accomplish it. We lose that feeling of helplessness and start to scheme how to obtain the results we want. If I were to make those sorts of bets, I think I would lose every time. Perhaps the best way to get quick results is to bribe your students outrageously.

We know that we learn best when we have actively selected the subject and have some control of the process. We need to consult students about repertoire and give them choices, not orders. We are helping them to build a more and more comprehensive reference system using the known as a jumping-off point for the unknown.

We know an atmosphere of authority and criticism makes us feel uncertain and resentful and is liable to produce either boring conformity or devious hostility.

Continuing criticism, discouragement, and focus on failure produces hopelessness, anger, and erodes self-confidence. Yet it still happens. Ideas have been instilled by the methods used to teach us in the first place. Teachers work in an institution that encourages an approach based on dubious assumptions about learners and teachers and a lack of trust in both. Anyone who operates under these ideas will have difficulty learning.

A teacher can pay attention, give protection, and respect each student for what he is and not criticise him for what he is not. He can also give both himself and his students permission to fail. No special effort is necessary.

The Homeopathic Music Workshop

Finally, I have an unfulfilled fantasy of running a workshop, or even summer school. It would be very different from those that are usually offered. Like Homeopathy, it would offer more of the same thing that was causing trouble in the first place. The tutors would be as rude and disparaging as possible and would take every opportunity to show off how good they were. They would be careful to mismatch predicates and body language. The tutors would help the students to get as poor a tone as possible and make sure they did not listen to it. (This would have to be done by not mentioning tone at all; actually telling them not to listen would have quite the opposite effect!)

Experienced orchestral players could teach ensembles

to be as sloppy and unrhythmic as possible without departing from the actual printed note values. Sightreading though, would have to be note perfect. All students would be taught to say "I can't" in individual lessons whenever they had any difficulties. This would be answered of course by the teacher saying "Well, you should".

Everyone would be told to practise several hours a day, taking as few breaks as possible. Gold stars would be given for effort and time spent, irrespective of result. All pieces would be monitored by metronome, and a prize would be given for the fastest rendition of a set piece. An Alexander teacher would be on hand to demonstrate a bad posture. Perfection would be constantly stressed and at the end of the course there would be a *very important* concert for as large an audience as possible. A winner would be announced onstage, based on audience clapometer ratings.

Looking back over this description, parts of it come uncomfortably close to what happens on some music courses. The crucial difference is that they do not see the joke. My course would be just as valuable, if not more so than a conventional one in terms of improving musical skills, although that would not be its direct purpose at all; if it was, it would lose its impact. Awareness is the answer. Knowing how to do something badly means knowing how to do it well. A choice is created. If you know what you are doing, and why you are doing it, you are free to change at will, and choose whatever you want.

Bibliography

F.M.Alexander   *The Use of Self*   Gollancz 1985

Richard Bandler and John Grinder *Frogs into Princes*
Real People Press 1979, *The Structure of Magic* Science and
Behaviour Books 1975, *The Structure of Magic II* Science and
Behaviour Books 1976

Gregory Bateson   *Steps Towards an Ecology of Mind*   Ballantine
Books 1972

T. Beaver and R. Chiarello   Cerebral Dominance in Musicians
and Non-Musicians, *Science* 185, 537-39

Evelyn I. Bird   Mental Rehearsal for Musicians, Theory,
Practice and Research *ISSTIP Journal* number 2, 1986

Gordon Bower Analysis of a Mnemonic Device *American Scientist*
58:504

John P. Briggs and F. David Peat   *Looking Glass Universe*
Fontana 1984

P.C. Buck   *Psychology for Musicians*   Oxford 1944

A. Buzan   *Use Both Sides of Your Brain*   Dutton 1977

Robert Dilts   *Roots of Neuro-Linguistic Programming*   Meta
Publications 1976, *Applications of Neuro-Linguistic Programming*
Meta Publications 1983

D. Delis, J. Fleer and P. Kerr   Memory for Music *Percept. and
Psychophys.* 23, 215-18, 1978

S. Dimond and J. Beaumont *Hemispheric Functions of the Human
Brain*   Paul Elek 1974

Betty Edwards   *Drawing on the Right Side of the Brain*
Tarcher, California, 1979

Hunter Fry   The Occupational Hazards of Musicianship
The Lancet,   September 1986

D. Galin and R. Ornstein   Individual Differences in Cognitive
Style-Reflective Eye Movements *Neuropsychologia* 1974, vol 12,
pp. 376-397

W. Timothy Gallwey   *The Inner Game of Tennis*   Random House
1974

M. Gazzaniga   *The Bisected Brain*   Appleton, Century and
Croft 1974

Michael Gelb   *Body Learning*   Aurum Press 1981

R.E. Gur, R.C. Gur, and L.J. Harris   Cerebral Activation as
Measured by Subject's Lateral Eye Movements, is Influenced by
Experimenter Location *Neuropsychologia* 13, (1975): 35-44

Ralph Haber   How We Remember What We See *Scientific
American*   May 1970, p.105

James Herndon   *How to Survive in Your Native Land*
Simon and Shuster New York 1971, *The Way It's spozed To be*
Simon and Shuster New York 1968

John Holt   *Freedom and Beyond*   Dutton 1972, *How Children
Learn*   Penguin 1967,   *Never Too Late*   Holt Associates 1984

Ivan Illich   *Deschooling Society*   Harper and Row 1970

E. Jacobsen   *Anxiety and Tension Control*   J.B. Lippincott,
Philadelphia 1964

M. Kinsbourne   Eye and Head Turning Indicates Cerebral
Lateralisation *Science* 179: 539-41 (1976)

D. Lauck   Winning Through Imagination *Mainliner*
March 1978, 48

B. Lewis and R.F. Pucelik *Magic Demystified* Metamorphous Press 1982

Jean Liedloff *The Continuum Concept* Futura 1976

William Lovelock *Common Sense in Music Teaching* Bell 1965

R.A. Magill *Motor Learning Concepts and Applications* W.C. Brown 1980

Alice Miller *The Drama of the Gifted Child* Faber and Faber 1979, *For Your Own Good* Faber and Faber 1980

George Miller The Magical Number Seven Plus or Minus Two *Psychological Review* 63:81-97

Robert Ornstein and Richard Thompson *The Amazing Brain* Chatto and Windus 1985

Kenneth Pelletier *Holistic Medicine* Dell, New York 1979

Fritz Perls *Gestalt Therapy Verbatim* Real People Press 1969

Neil Postman and Charles Weingartner *Teaching as a Subversive Activity* Penguin 1979

Karl Pribram *Languages of the Brain* Prentice-Hall 1974

J.W. Reitmeyer The Application of Negative Practice to the Correction of Habitual Fingering Errors in Clarinet Performance Unpublished Thesis, The Pennsylvania State University (Abstract in *Diss. Abstr. Int.* 1973, 33. 3403)

A. Richardson Mental Practice: A Review and Discussion *Research Quarterly* 38(1) and (2) 1967

Eloise Ristad *A Soprano on Her Head* Real People Press 1982

Carl Rogers *On Becoming a Person* Constable 1967, *Freedom to Learn for The 80's* Merrill 1983

R. Rosenthal and Leora Jacobsen   Teacher's Expectancies;
Determinants of Pupil's IQ Gains *Psychological reports* 19 (1):
115-118

Peter Russell   *The Brain Book*   Routledge and Kegan Paul 1979

Lee F. Ryan   *The Natural Classical Guitar*   Prentice-Hall 1984

Gerald Schuchman and Ernest Burgi   Report in the *Journal of
Auditory Research* Washington D.C.

O. C. Simonton, Matthews-Simonton and Creighton *Getting Well
Again*   Bantam New York 1980

John Sloboda   *The Musical Mind*   OUP 1985

Peter Shrag and Dianne Divoky *The Myth of the Hyperactive
Child*   Penguin 1981

Sally Springer and Georg Deutsch *Left Brain, Right Brain*
W.H Freeman & Co   New York   Revised Edition 1985

Richard Suinn Psychology and Sport Performance, Principles
and Applications in: R.M. Suinn (Ed)   *Psychology in Sports,
Methods and Applications*   Burgess 1980

Jeremy Williams   *The Effect of Composer Credibility on
Musical Preference*   unpublished thesis Keele University 1986

If you are interested in the ideas in this book, Lambent Books organises courses and seminars in a wide range of topics:

-Mental rehearsal

-Dealing with performance anxiety

-Practice methods

-Applications of NLP to music and education

-Use of language in education

Joseph O'Connor has written other books on NLP, including:
Principles of NLP (with Ian McDermott)
Introducing NLP (with John Seymour)
Training with NLP (with John Seymour)
Listening Skills in Music

For details of books and courses contact:

Joseph O'Connor
c/o Lambent Books
4 Coombe Gardens,
New Malden, Surrey
KT3 4AA
tel: 0181 715 2560